POVERTY
IN THE
PROMISED
LAND

POVERTY
IN THE
PROMISED
LAND

Neighborliness, Resistance,
and Restoration

Walter Brueggemann

Editor
Conrad L. Kanagy

Fortress Press
Minneapolis

POVERTY IN THE PROMISED LAND
Neighborliness, Resistance, and Restoration

29 28 27 26 25 24   1 2 3 4 5 6 7 8 9

Library of Congress Cataloging-in-Publication Data

Names: Brueggemann, Walter, author. | Kanagy, Conrad L., editor.
Title: Poverty in the promised land : neighborliness, resistance, and
   restoration / Walter Brueggemann ; editor, Conrad L. Kanagy.
Description: Minneapolis, MN : Fortress Press, [2024]
Identifiers: LCCN 2023059582 (print) | LCCN 2023059583 (ebook) | ISBN
   9798889831389 (print) | ISBN 9798889831396 (ebook)
Subjects: LCSH: Poverty--Biblical teaching. | Common good--Biblical
   teaching. | Bible--Criticism, interpretation, etc. | United
   States--Social conditions--21st century. | Desmond, Matthew.
Classification: LCC BS680.P47 B78 2024 (print) | LCC BS680.P47 (ebook) |
   DDC 261.8/325--dc23/eng/20240226
LC record available at https://lccn.loc.gov/2023059582
LC ebook record available at https://lccn.loc.gov/2023059583

Cover image: water droplets on glass window stock photo, from Derrykhrome-5/Unsplash
Cover design: LUCAS Art & Design, Jenison, MI

Print ISBN: 979-8-8898-3138-9
eBook ISBN: 979-8-8898-3139-6

for
the Jeff Haas Trio
and
Laurie Sears

The Jeff Haas Trio (Jack, Jeff, and Randy), and Laurie Sears on sax provide wondrous listening. But they do much more than that. Given Jeff's Jewish sensibility, through their music they probe the crevices of our sadness and loss, and they voice our best hope for new possibility. I am grateful to them for performing for Tia and me many luxurious hours of wellbeing and honesty.

CONTENTS

FOREWORD

Few people have shaped my theological imagination more than Walter Brueggemann. He is a legend, one of the most insightful biblical scholars of the past century . . . heck, maybe the past millennium. But this book is extra special. Not only do you get the brilliant hermeneutic of Dr. Brueggemann . . . you also get the profound social analysis of Pulitzer-prize-winning author Matthew Desmond, author of *Poverty, by America*. It's a divinely orchestrated literary cocktail of the best sort.

Karl Barth famously said that we need to read the Bible in one hand, and the newspaper in the other. He would love this book because that's exactly what you'll find. Our faith should never be used as a ticket into heaven and an excuse to ignore the world we live in. Too often, Christians have been so obsessed with heaven that we have ignored the hells people are living in right now. The good news is that God cares about this world. God cares about life before death, as well as life after death.

To be clear, this is a book about economics and poverty and greed, and systemic injustice, but it is also a book about Jesus and the gospel. It's a book about God's dream for the world, a dream that includes every person having everything they need to flourish. I remember Mother Teresa once saying that when God created the world, God did not mess up or make too many people or too little stuff. God created a perfect world. And we humans have made quite a mess of it. Poverty was not created by God but by us. We created it and we can end it, with the help of the Holy Spirit of course. That may sound audacious. But as you will find in the pages that follow, we have a God who makes all things possible . . . including ending poverty.

One of the most persistent themes in Scripture is that there is enough. There is enough for everyone's need, but not for everyone's greed. In sad irony, the enslaved Hebrew people made bricks, for the storehouses of Pharaoh in Egypt. They were building bricks for rich folks in an empire of inequity to stockpile riches for tomorrow while they did not have enough for today. And God rescued them. One of the first commands (even before the Ten Commandments) that God gives the Hebrew people who escaped Pharaoh's empire was this: only take what you need (Exod 16:1). When God rains down manna from heaven for food, God warns them if they take more than a day's ration, God will send maggots to eat up the surplus. They were also to take one omer of manna (about three pounds) as a symbol of their daily providence from God. It was about trust and about preventing greed and poverty.

We hear the subtle echo of it in the Lord's Prayer as we are taught to pray for "this day our daily bread." We see it in the mystery of the Eucharist as we break off a little for ourselves and pass it on. In fact, Paul scolds the early Christians for desecrating the Lord's table because some people were coming to the table hungry while others were gluttonous with their appetites. Paul makes it crystal clear in 2 Corinthians 8:15 as he promises that there will be enough for everyone if "the one who gathers will not gather too much." In God's dream, *there is enough* for everyone, if only we will share. We see that vision echoed in Proverbs: "Give me neither poverty nor riches but give me only my daily bread."

And we certainly see God's economy of abundance manifested in that first Pentecost as the early Christians held everything in common and shared their possessions with all those in need. The book of Acts even makes the audacious claim, "There were no needy persons among them" (Acts 4:34a). The early Church ended poverty. And so can we. That's the bold, faith-rooted proclamation you see in the pages that follow as Brueggemann builds on the work of Matthew Desmond. Nelson Mandela famously pointed out, "It always seems impossible until it's done." Before every social movement that has changed the world, many people said, "It's impossible!" And after that social movement people said, "It was inevitable." But history doesn't just happen—history is made. This book is a daring invitation to participate in making poverty history.

This book will also ruffle some feathers. That's what truth does. That's what the gospel does—comfort the disturbed and disturb the comfortable—because the gospel is *always* good news to the poor. If it is not good news to the poor, then it is not the gospel of Jesus.

There are over 2,000 verses of Scripture that speak about God's concern for the poor and call on us to advocate for the oppressed. One of the earliest visions we see in the gospel is the song of Mary, pregnant with Jesus in her womb: "The mighty will be cast down from their thrones, and the lowly will be lifted up. The hungry will be filled with good things, and the rich will be sent away empty" (Luke 1:52). That's not Karl Marx. That's the Gospel of Luke. And the gospel, I would suggest, is even more radical than Marx, or any form of socialism or communism. The gospel is about love, that harsh and dreadful love that Dostoevsky writes about. The love that keeps us up at night when we have an extra bed while our neighbor is sleeping on the streets. That love your neighbor as yourself kind of love that calls us to take action on behalf of the poor and dispossessed. That harsh and dreadful love that might even get us arrested or killed. That kind of love, that's what this book is about.

And that kind of love is a challenge to the status quo. We now live in a world where less than one hundred rich folks own the same amount of wealth as half the world (over 3.5 billion people!). Five billionaires now have more money than the combined economies of fifty countries. We have CEOs making five hundred times as much money as their workers. Sports stars make more money advertising shoes than all the combined salaries of the people in the sweatshops making those shoes. In a conservative estimate, Elon Musk alone, now the richest man in the world, makes over five hundred dollars per second, more than thirty thousand dollars per minute, and 46 million dollars a day. That's not a safe or sustainable world. The world will never be safe as long as millions of people live in desperate poverty while a handful of people have more than we can ever imagine. We've come a long way from God's dream for a world where everyone has enough and no one has too much.

This is why we have to talk about "systemic injustice." That's one of the threads you'll see all through this dazzling manifesto. God is making all things new . . . God is setting all things right. God is redeeming all that is broken, in us and in the world.

We find one of the earliest examples of biblically-based economic justice in Leviticus. The Jubilee is God's comprehensive unilateral restructuring of the community's assets. It was God's first reparations project—a systemic dismantling of inequality that was to happen in regular intervals as a remedy to systemic injustice and the unequal distribution of wealth (and poverty). As you will hear from Walter, the Jubilee was God's vision for releasing debt, setting enslaved people free, redistributing wealth, and caring for the earth. If only more Bible lovers and fundamentalists took the Jubilee literally! We would love in a different kind of world, one much closer to that world God designed where everyone has everything they need. There are those naysayers who point out that the Israelites never seem to have practiced the Jubilee . . . but a friend of mine says, "Christians have never really practiced the Sermon on the Mount either!" It was still God's command and God's vision for us. This book invites you to reimagine the Jubilee and to creatively interrupt injustice.

As followers of Jesus, we need compassion. Compassion is at the heart of the gospel. But compassion leads us to justice. Dr. Martin Luther King Jr. put it this way: we are all called to be the Good Samaritan and lift our neighbor out of the ditch on the road to Jericho. But after you lift so many people out of the ditch, you start to say, "We need to reimagine the road to Jericho!" Late Archbishop Desmond Tutu said, "There comes a point when we need to stop pulling people out of the river. We need to go upstream and find out why they are falling in." And these were the words of Dietrich Bonhoeffer who was executed for his opposition to the Nazis: "We are not to simply bandage the wounds of the victims beneath the wheels of injustice, we are to drive a spoke into the wheel itself."

We need to give people food. But we also have to ask why people are hungry, to begin with. My friend and mentor, Dr. John Perkins has a great take on the saying, "If you give someone a fish they will eat for a day. But if you teach them to fish, they will eat for the rest of their lives." He adds, "But we also have to do something about who owns the pond." Feeding people is compassion work, and it is holy . . . but making sure people have equal access to the pond is justice work, and it is also holy. Justice work requires being a prophetic force for life.

It's about going beyond just lifting people out of the ditch. It's about reimagining the road to Jericho. It's that prophetic imagination that Walter Brueggemann stirs in us so well, and it drips from the pages of this book.

Personal salvation and social transformation go hand-in-hand. They are like blades of scissors that work best when you hold them together. Or like the oars of a rowboat. Loving God and loving our neighbors are interconnected. God is personal and social. God is saving sinful individuals . . . and God is also redeeming a sin-filled world. The gospel is concerned with economic systems as well as saving souls. Jesus does not talk about pie-in-the-sky theological ideas, but he tells parables and stories about the stuff of earth—unjust judges, widows, day laborers, greedy bosses, and tireless vineyard workers. And nearly every time Jesus opens his mouth, he speaks about "the Kingdom of God," which is not just something we go up to when we die, but something we are to bring "on earth as it is in heaven." Surely, we see stories of personal salvation, like the one of a tax collector named Zacchaeus . . . but his transformation also manifests itself in economic transformation as he sells half of all his possessions and pays people back four times what he owed them. He did reparations, economic reparations.

God is up to something. God is redeeming the world. And God wants us to be a part of the revolution. God is inviting us to participate in the transformation of the world. God is challenging us not to get used to poverty, not to be comfortable with the suffering of our neighbors. God is daring us to reimagine the world.

This book reminds us that God's got a different dream than the American dream. God's dream is for every child to have food, shelter, and health care. God's dream is for every asylum seeker to find refuge and safety. God's dream is for the last to be first and the first to be last.

God's dream is for us to beat our weapons into farm tools and study war no more. Brueggemann, as always, invites us to dream with God, to conspire with God. We are not to conform to the empire in which we live; we are to be prophets of resistance, revolutionaries fueled by love.

I've been partners in ministry for over twenty years with my friend Tony Campolo. He's almost ninety years old now and had a stroke a few years back that slowed him down a little. But it didn't stop his dreams or get in the way of his vision for a better world. Tony often says, "We are as young as our dreams and as old as our cynicism." I heard him say that thirty years ago when I was an undergrad student at Eastern University. And then he would pause dramatically and get a huge, stubborn smile with a twinkle in his eyes and follow that line up with this one: "And I am younger than most of you . . . because you are so cynical."

Walter is now a little older than my pal Tony Campolo. He has crossed the ninety-year mark. But he is young. He is young because his dreams are so vivid and alive with hope, that hope rooted deeply in God's character and promises. He still knows how to dream and refuses to let cynicism wear him down.

Too much is at stake to become paralyzed by cynicism. So open your mind, soften your heart, and get ready for the ride. Here is the gospel, the good news of Jesus, which is always good news to the poor.

On a side note, I really hope I'm still writing books when I'm ninety years old. Thank you, Walter—you are a gift to the world and so is this book.

—Shane Claiborne, author of *The Irresistible Revolution, Beating Guns*, and, most recently, *Rethinking Life*

INTRODUCTION
History and Data Matter but so Does Theology

*The wolf shall live with the lamb, the leopard shall lie down
with the kid, the calf and the lion and the fatling together,
and a little child shall lead them. The cow and the bear shall
graze, their young shall lie down together, and the lion shall
eat straw like the ox. The nursing child shall play over the
hole of the asp, and the weaned child shall put its hand in
the adder's den. They will not hurt or destroy on all my holy
mountain; for the earth will be full of the knowledge of the
Lord as the waters cover the sea.*

—Isaiah 11:6–9

THIS IS THE fourth in a series of books that have emerged since May
2022, composed of short essays originally written as blog posts by
Walter Brueggemann from 2020 to the present. The essays reflect
Brueggemann at the top of his prophetic "game." It's hard to imagine
that like the wine of Jesus's first miracle, the best of Brueggemann
would be saved for the end of his days. But in essay after essay, I find
it hard to argue otherwise. In each, Walter brings to bear the biblical
exegetical method—for which he is so well known—to one contemporary social issue after another. No one else in the early part of the
twenty-first century is doing exactly this kind of contemporary theological and sociological reflection—and if they are, none as effectively,
honestly, and graciously as Brueggemann.

The man reads eight or nine books a week and two newspapers a day and has been doing so for decades. As a child, he read the *Christian Century* that his pastor father August didn't even read. He exhausted the small school library—causing the librarian to bring him books from town. Walter Brueggemann is a prolific writer in large part because he is a voracious reader. But not just any reader of any book. He is first and foremost a reader of the biblical text, and that text and its God have become the lens, or the frame, through which he sees, interprets, and prophetically imagines what God just might be up to that the rest of us haven't ever considered. Children and asps and adders in the nursery together? Wolves and lambs and lions and calves roaming the landscape eating from the same trough? In Walter's world—absolutely! For Brueggemann takes the biblical text as seriously as anyone I know, and because he believes the God of that text is free and sovereign, just anything might be possible.

Which is why I am so thankful for this book. Certainly, poverty has long been a concern of Brueggemann's and one about which he has written for decades. His son Jim remembers his dad watching the evening news and muttering about government policy toward the poor. But Walter had grown up hearing his parents mutter softly about the stinginess of congregations that paid their ministers so little but expected so much. Walter's father spent his two weeks of vacation each year working as a hired man on the western wheat harvest, earning more in two weeks than he did the rest of the year as a pastor. Walter grew up with a chip on his shoulder about the wealthy, or at least about those whose relative wealth created such inequities in his small town. The injustice came even closer home when his mother was slighted in the distribution of a sizeable family inheritance. Sparseness, scarcity, and saving were the realities of Walter's childhood.

But the injustice and lack of neighborliness extended beyond the church and Walter's family in the segregated Missouri town of Blackburn in which Walter grew up. Jim Crow was alive and well in Blackburn, and Walter and his brother Ed would receive permission from their father to attend the Black church across town—an early expression of resistance to the segregation by race and income that he witnessed. One of Walter's first jobs was helping to clean the separate but definitely not equal segregated Black school. While Walter was aware of the relative deprivation of his family, he soon learned that the continuum of poverty extended more deeply into the Black community and beyond his own circumstances. The chip on Walter's shoulder about poverty and inequality was one that he carried not only for himself but for the poor and marginalized of all colors and statuses and identities.

Neighborliness has been a theme of Brueggemann's through much of his work, and is directly related he would say, to the simple faith of the German Evangelical Pietism by which he was formed, and the irenic Christian expression that sought to minimize the quarrels of the Old World and to reflect the simple gospel truth of the New Commandment of Jesus to love God and neighbor. Indeed, it was the commitment to "in essentials unity, in non-essentials liberty, and in all things charity" that guided the formation of Walter Brueggemann (*Walter Brueggemann's Prophetic Imagination*, Fortress Press, 2024: 53). When I asked Walter in March 2022 what he wanted his biography to reveal, he immediately responded that he had not moved far from the German Evangelical Pietism of his youth. And in fact, one only needs to reread his more than one hundred books to see that this simple gospel message of love for God and neighbor has guided nearly everything that Walter has written, preached, and taught. In embracing the marginalized, Walter was embraced by progressives in the church. But many missed the deep theological commitments that grounded his values in the biblical text. Many evangelicals rejected Walter's progressive social agenda and like progressives, failed to see that it was his serious commitment to the Scripture that guided that agenda. He has frequently told me that he has no time for social justice efforts or advocacy that fail to ground themselves within the biblical text and the God of that text who forever loves and seeks after the poor and marginalized. Walter's commitment to justice for the poor is fully saturated in the love of God for all people.

Despite the bitter memories of the church's treatment of his father, Walter still loves the church. At ninety years of age, he has seen its ugly underside from just about every position and angle that one can imagine. When I asked him why, he said, "Because it is the only entity that still carries the Story and because where the church is functioning well, the neighborhood is thriving." Many have missed the fact that Walter Brueggemann's message was a missional one long before missional came along with its expert consultants, sophisticated techniques for getting pew dwellers out into the neighborhood, and expensive workshops with big-name speakers. No, missional for Brueggemann was always the gospel and the gospel was always missional. And like all things gospel, love for the neighbor was simple and not complex. Even a despised Samaritan could do it when the church leader on his way to a missional committee meeting could not.

What I love about this particular book as both pastor and sociologist, is that Brueggemann takes a sophisticated and sound analysis of poverty in America (in this case *by* America) from sociologist Matthew Desmond, a Pulitzer-prize winning author for his work on eviction in the United States, and overlays it with the prophetic imagination

for which he is so well known. Walter once told me that his herme-
neutical approach is simple—study the biblical text for its historical
movements and realities, add sociology to the mix, and then on top of
it all add a theological perspective that ties together God's activity in
the biblical text with God's activity today. In this book, Brueggemann
gives us a treat that Desmond alone doesn't and can't offer us.

Desmond sets out to do something a bit different than others
with his book. He acknowledges that many books have been written
with an eye to the conditions of the poor but that too few have trained
their eyes on the structural difficulties and systemic sources of poverty
in America that were intentionally created and remained sustained
by those with wealth. He presents the latest data which is even more
discouraging than it was sixty years ago for those of us who want to
see greater equity in America. He makes no bones about the fact that
the Republican party has the worst record of addressing poverty as
compared to those on the left. But he also minces no words for progressives who talk a good game, but play by the same rules as those on the
right. Rules that protect their self-interest, property, investments, and
power. There is something to offend everyone in his book.

Desmond's solutions to poverty are right on the mark. Besides
policy changes and structural redistribution about which I am somewhat cynical of becoming reality anytime soon, Desmond settles on
neighborliness as a possible answer to the chasm between rich and
poor, white and Black and brown, and the multiple sources of segregation and inequality that divide our nation and its people. And this
is where Brueggemann greets Desmond's analysis of poverty with a
hearty "amen" and then does what no one else can do. He takes us on
a journey across the biblical canon to remind us that neighborliness is
indeed godliness! Since our breakup with Yahweh in Eden, God has

been at work to repair the bridges that keep us from one another, to tear down the fences and walls of our selfish social construction, and to build smooth highways that take all of creation into the presence of God (Isa 40). We visit a mountain where it is imaginable that lions and lambs and children and adders just might be neighbors after all. And perhaps even rich and poor, Black, brown, and white, Republican and Democrat, atheist and believer. And the beauty of Walter Brueggemann is that he believes this can be the case sooner rather than later among the saints in Blackburn, Detroit, Philadelphia, and wherever the good earth still belongs to the Lord and where the presence of the Lord covers the earth as waters cover the sea.

Like Brueggemann, Desmond was a pastor's kid and victim of the subjective and arbitrary choices of wealthier folks in the church. And like Brueggemann, he resented the relative poverty that his father's occupation brought to his family. From time to time, theological echoes float alongside Desmond's keen sociological analysis. Desmond and Brueggemann are also alike in their assumption that the social world has been constructed in such a way as to favor the wealthy and privileged. Poverty is not coincidental with human societies but rather the product of a conspiracy of the powerful to retain their benefits and status. But both Brueggeman and Desmond argue that a socially constructed world that supports power can also be deconstructed to create a world of equity and justice.

Desmond's first choice for deconstructing the old and renovating a new world is related to new policy and political initiatives. But he also does it from the perspective of neighborliness, and imagining that a nation of neighbors might together tear down the national divide by being neighborly to those around us. Desmond spends substantial time pointing out that the segregation of our neighborhoods is by income and economics—not just by race. But the sheer fact that we are segregated by income and wealth, necessarily means we are segregated by race because of the historic oppression of Black and brown at every level of American society.

Brueggemann embraces the fundamental thesis of Desmond as he has since he discovered liberation theology in the early 1970s and began to embrace a conflict perspective of America's stratified society. But Brueggemann departs from Desmond by bringing the biblical text to the table, showing us that poverty in our neighborhoods is not a new problem or an American problem, but a human problem. It is also a problem for the people of God to address. It is a problem of the church's mission failure.

Thus, this book is a wake-up call to the church that has so cloaked itself in the last two decades in missional language, missional programs, missional this, and missional that. Still, church attendance continues to decline, our children continue to abandon the church, and the church is growing ever grayer. But as always Brueggemann offers a biblical perspective and solution that is never beyond our reach if we are the people of God who worship the God of the biblical text. Like the people of God in Babylonian captivity, if we offer shalom to those around us, shalom will come back to visit us at the end of the day. And where there is shalom in our neighborhoods there will also be enough food and drink and shelter and friendship to go around. But only if we keep giving shalom away to our neighbors.

I've given this little book the title *Poverty in the Promised Land: Neighborliness, Resistance, and Restoration* because the biblical story of Israel's exodus from Egypt to the promised land has long been the favored focus of Brueggemann. The movement from slavery to freedom. From have not to have it all. From enmity to reconciliation.

From judgment to grace. From rigor to welcome. All divine pivots that move us closer to a home where all are welcomed, all are free, all are equal, all are loved, and all are God's children. Alas, Brueggemann often acknowledges the failure of God's people in the promised land to fulfill Yahweh's commands about neighborliness or the church's failure to follow Jesus's second of the greatest commandments.

And likewise, in the United States, a nation that from the very beginning was considered by its European conquerors to be the promised land all over again, the same story of death and destruction to the poor and marginalized was repeated. It would become a promised land only to those who promised their lives to the powerful. To those who in God's name promised themselves to the highest bidder. To those who would abandon the red letters of the Sermon on the Mount and promise themselves to Wall Street, Walmart, and border walls between haves and have-nots. In the Old Testament, Brueggemann points to Solomon's reign as the undoing of God's design for a regular resetting of freedom and redistribution of wealth. In the early twenty-first century, he continues to point to capitalism as the mechanism of slavery, inequality, and injustice.

Both Desmond and Brueggemann make it clear that there is no promise in America for the poor and marginalized unless the divide between the two is tackled at the level of neighbor to neighbor. Unless we walk across the hall, the street, the porch, the bridge and look eye-to-eye with the other we've objectified and, in doing so, open ourselves to unknown outcomes where the Spirit's movement is most likely to thrive. And this is the gift of Brueggemann who constantly reminds us that we are in God's story and that this God is free and unpredictable and unknown. This God comes in from behind and underneath and usually takes us by surprise. This God is not constrained by our socially constructed categories, by gated communities, by border walls, by railroad tracks, by Babel, by the one percent, or by anything else we've created to keep out others but that has also kept out God. This God is making all things new! Now, not later. And the choice Brueggemann leaves us with is whether we get in the game and work with the Spirit's dismantling of segregation or whether we continue to work against the Spirit!

And the one who was seated on the throne said, "See, I am making all things new." Also he said, "Write this, for these words are trustworthy and true." (Rev 21:5)

Conrad L. Kanagy, Editor

❦ 1 ❦

TAKING

IT IS UNAMBIGUOUSLY clear to me that the church, at a local level, must address the matter of *systemic economic injustice* among us. I can think of two reasons why that responsibility falls on the church. First, almost all of the potentially critical voices concerning the economy have, to some great extent, accepted the assumptions of confiscatory capitalism. It is so for much of university culture, and it is so for the media. The church gets the assignment by default. But a second, more important reason is that economic justice is at the heart of a gospel ethic. This has been so since Moses, propelled by the liberating God, Yahweh, emancipated the slaves from Pharaoh's predatory slave economy. When Moses performed that liberation, he authorized *an alternative economy* committed to debt forgiveness via the Torah provisions for "the Year of Release" (Deut 15:1–18) and the Jubilee Year (Lev 25). My thinking in this direction has been greatly fueled by Matthew Desmond, *Poverty, by America* (2023). Desmond, the Pulitzer Prize-winning author of *Evicted*, explores both the causes and the outcomes of a predatory economy that willfully produces and sustains a poverty class of those who are victims of impossible debt and thus a pool for cheap labor. My several reflections on the theme are triggered by my reading of Desmond.

My first appeal to Desmond concerns his recognition that we live in a usurpative economy of *aggressive taking*:

> *It's a useful exercise, evaluating the merits of different*
> *explanations for poverty, like those having to do with*
> *immigration or the family. But I've found that doing so*
> *always leads me back to the taproot, the central feature from*
> *which all other rootlets spring, which in our case is the simple*
> *truth that poverty is an injury, a taking. Tens of millions*
> *of Americans do not end up poor by a mistake of history or*
> *personal conduct. Poverty persists because some wish and will*
> *it to.* (p. 40)

Desmond's book overflows with data concerning the way our economic system operates to the continuing advantage of some at the expense of others. The accent on "taking" is an insistence that the gap between haves and have-nots is not happenstance; nor is it because of the failure of the have-nots. Rather, it is the intended outcome of a system that intends to deliver gains for those who already have an overflowing abundance.

Desmond's stark accent on "taking" has caused me to reflect on the great drama of "taking" that is staged in the history of Israel and in the larger world which ancient Israel inhabited. I will cite a sufficient number of textual examples to indicate that *an economy of taking* is pervasive in that ancient world, and to consider the way in which ancient Israel is summoned, from the outset, to practice an economy that is not preoccupied with taking, but rather with prospering according to an embrace of the common good.

Of course, Israel did not invent an economy of taking. K. C. Hanson writes to me that Assyriologist Karen Radner has shown how Neo-Assyrian evidence suggests loans at 12 percent to 40 percent per month. Israel had immediately before it highly compelling models for such systemic coercive taking, notably that of Pharaoh, from whose "taking" they had escaped. We have a quick summary of Pharaoh's acquisitive policies in Genesis 47:13–26. The narrative begins with the recognition that Pharaoh had a monopoly on food, thus his expansive granaries. The peasant farmers were at his mercy during the famine. It is reported that in the first year of the famine, Joseph, on behalf of Pharaoh, "collected" (*lqt*) all the money of the peasants (v. 14). That is, Pharaoh sold the needy peasants grain from his monopoly. In the second year when the peasants had no more money with which to purchase grain, Pharaoh traded the needed grain for their livestock (v. 17). He took their horses, flocks, herds, and donkeys, that is, their means of production. He put them out of business and made them even more dependent on his monopoly. In the third wave of their unrelieved need, they came in their need to Pharaoh empty-handed. As with all such predators, it did not occur to Pharaoh to be generous with the peasants. He was insistent on an uncompromising quid pro quo from them. The peasants understood very well, and so they said:

> *Buy us and our land in exchange for food. We with our land will become slaves to Pharaoh; just give us seed, so that we may live and not die, and that the land may not become desolate.* (v. 19)

Their request is one of desperation. And so, *their land* was transferred to Pharaoh. And *their bodies* were reduced to slave status. They had no other bargaining leverage. They are relieved to be alive at all:

> *You have saved our lives; may it please my lord, we will be slaves to Pharaoh.* (v. 25)

It will be noted that in each of these transactions, the matter is according to the strict rules of trade, so that there is no coercion or cheating. It is only the hard-nosed reality of economic transactions between haves and have-nots, when there is no room for compassion or generosity. Thus,

- Joseph *collected* all the money. (v. 14)
- Joseph gave them food *in exchange* for their horses, their flocks, their herds, and their donkeys. He exchanged food for livestock. (v. 17)
- Joseph bought all the land of Egypt for Pharaoh. (v. 20)
- Joseph made slaves of the peasant people. (v. 21)

The verbs are telling: "collect," "give in exchange," "bought." Every act is a market transaction. That is, the acts are without any hint of exploitation, beyond the exploitation that is intrinsic in transactions between haves and have-nots. Pharaoh is narrated as a ruthless trader with an insatiable appetite for more. It is likely that he was not better or worse than any of his contemporary counterparts, all of whom together constituted the economic horizon into which the Israelite "covenantal revolution" was situated. That "covenantal revolution" that intended neighborly transactions was very upstream in such a quid pro quo world. Precisely for that reason Moses, in his climactic command-ment to Israel, prohibits "coveting" that is the propulsion for Pharaoh's accumulative policies (see Exod 20:17).

It is not any great wonder then that Israel should be sharply aware of the acquisitive world all around, and should be attentive to its urgent pursuit of accumulation in the interest of security and comfort. Soon enough Israel would face a crisis as it adjudicated between this "normative" monetary system, and its own alternative vision. That adjudication comes into clear focus as Israel entertains the prospect of establishing a monarchy in order to be "like the nations" with its own security system.

The advocates of monarchy saw the advantages of such an arrangement and did not pause at all to notice how it would represent a deep contradiction to their covenantal commitments. The matter was left to Samuel, seer and judge, to make clear. Early on in the struggle toward a viable adequate government, Samuel, from his covenantal perspective, found the monarchy to be an act of service to other gods (1 Sam 8:8). It is not simply a political act of self-assertion on the part of Israel, but a perverse theological act that violates the very character of Israel. Samuel knew enough of the royal model to see that it sponsored and required an alternative articulation of justice:

This will be the justice of the king *who will reign over you.*

(v. 11; emphasis added)

A new offer of quid pro quo justice will displace the restorative justice of neighborly generosity:

The king will take *your sons and daughters* (v. 11);

The king will appoint *them to his chariots and to be his horse-men* (v. 11);

The king will appoint *them to be his commanders, his farmers, and his weapons smithies* (v. 12);

The king will take *your daughters* (v. 12);

The king will take *the best of your fields, vineyards, and orchards* (v. 14);

> *The king will* take *10% of your produce* (v. 15);
> *The king will* take *your male and female slaves* (v. 16);
> *The king will* take *the best of your cattle and donkeys* (v. 16);
> *The king will* take *10 percent of your flocks . . .*
> *You shall be his slaves* (v. 17)!

This speech by Samuel anticipates that the more covenantal Israel imitates the other nations, the more it will compromise its covenantal identity and participate in the economic predation of the powerful against the vulnerable.

The evidence on King David is somewhat mixed. He is remembered as one who acted in genuine solidarity with his people and especially with his troops (see 2 Sam 23:13–17). However, in one particular dramatic way, David acts with the "taking" anticipated in Samuel's speech. In 2 Samuel 11, it is reported concerning David:

> *So David sent messengers and he* took *her [Bathsheba], and she came to him.* (2 Sam 11:4)

It is worth noting that the verb "take" is the same verb that reverberated in Samuel's attestation. It is equally worth notice that the NRSV glides over the verb with an innocuous "to get her." The verb is much more direct and much more aggressive, bespeaking the king's capacity and readiness to seize the woman for his satisfaction. He is sufficiently a "taker" to evoke the harsh response of Nathan (2 Sam 12:1–15).

While the data on David is ambiguous, there is no such ambiguity concerning his son, Solomon, who is the premier "taker" in ancient Israel. The expansive opulence of Solomon's urban environment bespeaks his capacity to seize resources as he chose. In addition to his aggressive trade policies, we may notice that his immense wealth is derived from two principal sources. First, he developed a *tax collecting system* whereby he seized the agricultural produce of the peasant economy (1 Kgs 4:7–19). The harshness of his tax system may be reflected in the tax revolt reported in 1 Kings 12:1–19. While the revolt had to wait until his death, there is no doubt that the seeds of resentment and peasant unrest had been long germinating during his reign. Second, Solomon relied on *cheap labor* which in his case was state slavery. The text suggests, ambiguously, that his slave force was constituted only by foreigners or by both foreigners and Israelites (1 Kgs 5:13, 9:15–22). Either way, the system was expansively exploitative. But then, this is exactly what "taking" looks like, the forcible appropriation of resources of the vulnerable and reliance on cheap labor from the vulnerable who are too weak and impotent to resist such exploitation. The combination of these two practices is a surefire path to economic wealth!

Finally, we may notice that the Omri dynasty in Northern Israel—and more specifically King Ahab, son of Omri—provided an echo and counterpoint to the predatory practice of Solomon. In the paradigmatic narrative of 1 Kings 21, the royal couple—Ahab and Jezebel—preys upon the "inheritance" of Naboth, a peasant farmer. As the land is his "inheritance," it is not available for the brash commoditization to which the royal house was committed. The royal couple, however, is undeterred by that old-fashioned peasant reluctance. Their quest for land is without satiation, and so in its violent way, the throne acts to seize the property. The narrative report of the seizure of Naboth's inheritance is inflected by the double use of the term "possess," a term bespeaking coercive force:

> *As soon as Jezebel heard that Naboth had been stoned and*
> *was dead, Jezebel said to Ahab, "Go, take possession of the*
> *vineyard of Naboth the Jezreelite, which he refused to give*
> *you for money; for Naboth is not alive, but dead." As soon as*
> *Ahab heard that Naboth was dead, Ahab set out to go down*
> *to the vineyard of Naboth the Jezreelite, to take possession of*
> *it.* (1 Kgs 21:15–16)

The land has been successfully converted, in an instant of reformulation, from "inheritance" to "property." The royal house has accomplished its greedy, predatory goal. Except, what follows in the narrative is a critical reprise on behalf of Naboth by the prophet, Elijah:

> *Have you killed and also taken possession . . . Thus says the*
> *Lord: In the place where dogs licked up the blood of Naboth,*
> *dogs will also lick up your blood.* (v. 19)

The two verbs of the prophet readily go together: "kill" and possess." *Kill* if necessary to *possess!*

The church, along with the synagogue, has this textual tradition of "taking" entrusted to it. The avoidance of economic matters in the church has caused the systematic neglect of this textual tradition in the church that has in turn legitimated silence in the church on such issues. For the most part, we in the church have had nothing to say about how the powerful take from the vulnerable. The practice of "taking" is propelled by the powerful who exercise massive influence on economic policy in our society. As a result, tax policy, interest rates, wage rates, and much of governmental largess are regulated according to the gains and interests of the wealthy. The problem is made more acute for the church through the fact that many of us in the church are not wealthy, but benefit from the same exploitative policies. Thus when the church speaks out on these issues, the church is sure to find itself, as a body, in profound conflict.

Given that undoubted social reality, it is nonetheless the case that the biblical tradition places the *crisis of money* at the very center of gospel faith. And while many pastors and congregations are not prepared to be frank about the matter, at a very minimum we may do the work that makes these texts available in the church, so that church members are able to see the crisis of "taking" as not only a crisis in our society but as a core crisis in our textual tradition. It is not for nothing that Moses's Ten Commandments concludes with a terse prohibition: "Thou shalt not covet" (Exod 20:17). The prohibition specifically refers to wives, slaves, oxen, and donkeys. In order not to be misunderstood it ends with an all-inclusive "anything." The scope of the commandment is not petty acts of envy. It is on policy questions that regulate (or fail to regulate) economic transactions between the powerful and the vulnerable.

Imagine that in an economy propelled by "takers" the church holds to the conviction that "giving" and not "taking" is the clue to common well-being. The church has a stake in *policies of giving*, whereby the resources of the community are made available according to need in every sphere of life. Thus, the church has a stake in policies in response to needs concerning health, housing, education, and all else that brings shared well-being. The practical memory of the church has concerned itself with such matters since the narrative of Acts 5:1–11 concerning the management of wealth. The sorry tale of Ananias and

Sapphira is a continuing tale about how "taking" damages the whole body, that is, to the body politic. The news is that it need not be so. Our economy can indeed be done differently! We may heed the notice of the narrator of the story in Acts:

> *And great fear seized the whole church and all who heard of these things.* (Acts 5:11)

⚜ 2 ⚜

DEVOURING

MY SECOND APPEAL to Desmond concerns his compelling use of the imagery of "devouring" in *Poverty, by America* whereby agents of strength prey upon the vulnerable with an aggressive and insatiable appetite. Desmond quotes from Stephen Sondheim, in his dark musical *Sweeney Todd*:

> *The history of the world, my sweet—is who gets eaten and*
> *who gets to eat* (Poverty, by America, 42).

The imagery of "devouring" strikes one as a forceful and fierce way of characterizing a dog-eat-dog enterprise in which the vulnerable are completely at the mercy of the insatiable appetite and irrepressible aggression of the powerful. The imagery bespeaks, for Desmond, a drive that is ruthless, irresistible, and endlessly hungry and in pursuit of "more." Desmond's chapter 3, in which the imagery occurs, is entitled, "How We Undercut Workers." The chapter details how defenseless workers are slotted for poor pay and evaporating benefits. Desmond, moreover, traces the predictable effect of such exploitation in the savaging of the health and quality of life of such victims of the "devouring."

Both the imagery and the subject matter of Desmond have caused me to consider the counterpoint to Desmond's analysis in Scripture. The following texts come to mind.

1. A most representative wisdom saying is offered in Proverbs:

> *There are those whose teeth are swords,*
> *whose teeth are knives,*
> to devour the poor *from off the earth,*
> *the needy from among mortals.* (Prov 30:14)

The saying concerns those who are "pure in their own eyes" (v. 11), who are "lofty in their own eyes" (v. 13), and who act in covetous ways, even against their own father and mother. Such persons are judged to be endlessly self-serving, who will stop at nothing for their advancement and prosperity. Given such insatiable urges, it is not a surprise that with teeth like sharp weapons, they can bite off, chew, and spit out everyone and everything. Predictably, such greedy self-assertion easily treats the "poor and needy" as easy and disposable victims, so as to devour them on their hurried way to more wealth and power.

The wisdom saying does not trace out what the positive counterpoint to such savagery might be. We can, however, imagine that it includes a settled practice in the village, with due regard and respect for one's parents, and a sense of solidarity with and responsibility for the poor and needy in the community. We get such a portrayal of solidarity in the self-validation speech of Job in chapter 31. Job asserts, concerning the poor:

> *If I have withheld anything that the poor desired,*
> *or have caused the eyes of the widow to fail,*
> *or have eaten my morsel alone,*
> *and the orphan has not eaten from it—*
> *for from my youth I reared the orphan like a father,*

and from my mother's womb I guided the widow—
if I have seen anyone perish for lack of clothing,
or a poor person without covering,
whose loins have not blessed me,
and who has not warmed with the fleece of my sheep;
if I have raised my hand against the orphan,
because I saw I had supporters at the gate;
then let my shoulder blade fall from my shoulder,
and let my arm be broken from its socket.
For I was in terror of calamity from God,
and I could not have faced his majesty. (Job 31:16–23)

Those who are critiqued in our proverb and by Desmond have no such compunction about social responsibility or solidarity as does Job. Job is a person of *social solidarity* just as the foolish person in our proverb is not; they imagine that every person is on their own to make it as best as they can. That foolish person is a model for the ones who "devour" in the script of Desmond. By contrast, Job in his innocence embodies the counter-practice that yields protection and resources for the poor and needy who are seen to be members of Job's own community and village.

2. An oracle of condemnation in Ezekiel may be taken as a measure of prophetic indignation concerning the devouring of the vulnerable. The oracle proceeds, step by step, through the power structure of Jerusalem:

- Its princes
    within it are like a roaring lion tearing the prey; they have devoured *human lives; they have taken treasure and precious things; they have made many widows within it.* (Ezek 22:25)

- Its priests
  have done violence to my teaching and have profaned my holy
  things; they have made no distinction between the holy and
  the common, neither have they taught the difference between
  the unclean and the clean, and they have disregarded my
  sabbaths, so that I am profaned among them. (v. 26)

- Its officials
  within it are like wolves tearing the prey, shedding blood,
  destroying lives to get dishonest gain. (v. 27)

- Its prophets
  have smeared whitewash on their behalf, seeing false visions
  and divining lies for them. (v. 28)

- The people of the land
  have practiced extortion and committed robbery; they have
  oppressed the poor and needy, and have extorted from the
  alien without redress. (v. 29)

The exact indictment varies in each case according to the function of
the office:

> *Princes . . . by taxation*
> *Priests . . . by disregard of Sabbath*
> *Officials . . . like wolves for savage gain*
> *Prophets . . . by lies and distortions*
> *The community . . . by aggression and extortion*

Daniel Block, in *The Book of Ezekiel Chapters 1–24*, page 724, calls our attention to the way in which Ezekiel utilizes the earlier oracle by Zephaniah:

> *The officials within it are like roaring lions;*
> *its judges are evening wolves that leave nothing until the*
>   *morning.*
> *Its prophets are reckless, faithless persons;*
> *its priests have profaned what is sacred,*
> *they have done violence to the law.* (Zeph 3:3–4)

Given these variations of function, it is all of a piece. All members of the urban power structure participate together in the abuses and betrayals of the vulnerable who, in Ezekiel 22:29, are readily identified as the "poor and needy," exactly the same as in the proverb cited above.

3. In a later Ezekiel text the prophet asserts a hope that it does not need to be this way, exactly the hope of Desmond's book (Ezek 36:13–15). In verse 13, the harsh charge against Israel is reiterated yet again:

> *You* devour *people, and you bereave your nation of children.*
> (v. 13)

But then the following verses dare imagine otherwise when the savage devouring is stopped. The alternative of verses 14–15 reflects the larger anticipation of Ezekiel for a radical new beginning in Israel, including a new shepherd (v. 34), a new covenant (v. 36), and a new temple (v. 40–48).

Here the clue is the five-fold reiteration of "no longer" (*lo' 'od*):

No longer devouring *people;*
no longer *bereaving your nation of children;*
no longer *hearing the insults of the nations;*
no longer *bearing the disgrace of the peoples;*
no longer *shall you cause your nation to stumble.*
    (Ezek 36:14–15)

The prophetic "no longer" is an expectation and an assurance that the old regime of "devouring" need no longer continue and will not continue.

The same contrast of old practice and new possibility is articulated in Ezekiel's mandate to Israel's "shepherds" (rulers). The old shepherds were fully and without restraint self-serving:

> *You eat the fat, you clothe yourselves with the wool, you*
> *slaughter the fatlings; but you do not feed the sheep. You have*
> *not strengthened the weak, you have not healed the sick, you*
> *have not bound up the injured, you have not brought back*
> *the strayed, you have not sought the lost, but with force and*
> *harshness you have ruled them.* (Ezek 34:3–4)

But now the prophet can anticipate a new beginning with a radically different social practice when power is deployed according to the intent of the Lord God:

> *I will feed them with good pasture, and the mountain heights*
> *of Israel shall be their pasture; there they shall lie down in*

good grazing land and they shall feed on rich pasture on the
mountains of Israel. I myself will be the shepherd of my sheep,
and I will make them lie down, says the Lord God. I will
seek the lost, and I will bring back the strayed, and I will
bind up the injured, and I will strengthen the weak, but the
fat and the strong I will destroy. I will feed them with justice.
(Ezek 34:14–16)

Feeding them instead of *devouring* them! The prospect of a future in which God, the shepherd, rules directly is brought down to political reality in verses 23–24 by the anticipation of a new David who will be very different from the old exploitative regime:

I will set over them one shepherd, my servant David, and
he shall feed them; he shall feed them and be their shepherd.
And I, the Lord, will be their God, and my servant David
shall be prince among them; I, the Lord, have spoken.
(Ezek 34:23–24)

Not unlike Desmond, Ezekiel makes a clear, decisive distinction between present exploitation and a new future well-being that features restorative relationships instead of those of commoditization.

4. One other prophetic text claims our attention because it mentions "eating the flesh of my people":

Listen, you heads of Jacob and rulers of the house of Israel!
Should you not know justice?—
you who hate the good and love the evil,

who tear the skin off my people,
and the flesh off their bones;
who eat the flesh *of my people,*
flay their skin off them,
break their bones in pieces,
and chop them up like meat in a kettle,
like flesh in a caldron. (Mic 3:1–3)

The imagery of butchering and cooking human bodies is more elaborate here. The described brutality is contrasted to "justice," and the "hate of good and the love of evil" is the exact contrast to the saying of Amos:

Hate evil and love good,
and establish justice in the gate. (Amos 5:15)

The imagery of "devouring" is filled out with indicting specificity in other words of Micah:

They covet fields, and seize them,
houses, and take them away;
they oppress householder and house,
people and their inheritance. (Mic 2:2)

Hear this, you rulers of the house of Jacob
and chiefs of the house of Israel,
who abhor justice and pervert all equity,
who build Zion with blood and Jerusalem with wrong!
Its rulers give judgment for a bribe,
its priests teach for a price,

its prophets give oracles for money;
yet they lean upon the Lord and say,
"Surely the Lord is with us!
No harm shall come upon us." (Mic 3:9–11)

The faithful have disappeared from the land,
and there is no one left who is upright;
they all lie in wait for blood,
and they hunt each other with nets.
Their hands are skilled to do evil;
the official and judge ask for a bribe,
and the powerful dictate what they desire;
thus they pervert justice. (Mic 7:2–3)

The sum of this imagery is economic exploitation as the way in which the poor, needy, and vulnerable are cooked and eaten.

5. Finally, we may cite one teaching of Jesus that is an echo of the imagery we have found in both sapiential and prophetic texts. Jesus condemns the scribes who love their social visibility and who strut around the synagogue and at the best dinners:

As he taught, he said, "Beware of the scribes, who like to walk
around in long robes, and to be greeted with respect in the
marketplaces, and to have the best seats in the synagogues and
places of honor at banquets! They devour widows' houses and
for the sake of appearance say long prayers. They will receive
the greater condemnation. (Mark 12:38–40; see Luke 20:45–47)

Only in verse 40 does the report provide specificity about the work of the scribes that abuse the vulnerable. Again we have the word, "devour," with the object, "widows' houses." The scribes were the legal experts who, by filling out a form, could have property transferred. In this passage the scribes anticipate the "men with clipboards" in John Steinbeck's *The Grapes of Wrath*. When they write something down, an Okie has lost more property. So with the scribes. When they write something down, the vulnerable are more disadvantaged and impoverished. Their acquisitive action against the poor is a perfect counterpoint to their high visibility among the elite of Jerusalem. It is for good reason that in the next paragraph of Mark, a "poor widow" is noticed (Mark 12:41–44). She is a contrast to "many rich people" who give large sums of money to the temple treasury. They could afford it, precisely because of exploitation of the poor. All the while they are men of great piety, praying long prayers! The parallel in Matthew 23:1–12 makes their condemnation more inclusive and less precise, but it does refer to an imposition of "heavy burdens," likely the tax system that was a special liability for the poor. Our key term, "devour," has disappeared from Matthew's presentation, but the same inference can be drawn from his verses.

The sum of all these texts is the unbearable economic burden the powerful have placed upon the vulnerable, a burden so demanding that it robs the poor of a chance of a livable life. The chapter in which Desmond uses the term "devour" is entitled, "How We Undercut Workers." In it we are offered an illuminating discussion of a "minimum wage," union-busting to rob labor of negotiating leverage, the reduction of work to "gig jobs" that provide no security, and the formation of an economic class labeled as "the precarity," those who live endlessly in an economically precarious situation.

The Bible, since the Exodus emancipation, has been concerned with fair employment practices. In a Torah teaching, it is provided that workers must be paid on the day of their earning:

> *You shall not withhold the wages of poor and needy laborers, whether other Israelites or aliens who reside in your land in one of your towns. You shall pay them their wages daily before sunset, because they are poor and their livelihood depends on them; otherwise they might cry out to the Lord against you, and you would incur guilt.* (Deut 24:14–15)

We may take this provision as a more general requirement that workers must be treated fairly, because the Lord to whom they cry in their injustice is the great enforcer of workers' rights. In a much later text, Jeremiah condemns King Jehoiakim for his predatory labor practice:

> *Woe to him who builds his house by unrighteousness,*
> *and his upper rooms by injustice;*
> *who makes his neighbors work for nothing,*
> *and does not give them their wages.* (Jer 22:13)

The king makes his subjects work "for nothing," and does not give them their pay. The indictment sounds like a reiteration of the state labor policy of King Solomon, a practice he had perhaps learned in turn from Pharaoh!

At the conclusion of his chapter, Desmond reiterates in a mocking way the common popular advice given to poor people:

> *The poor should change their behavior to escape poverty.* Get
> a better job. Stop having children. Make smarter financial
> decisions. (62)

But Desmond contradicts that easy dismissive advice, and asserts to
the contrary:

> *In truth, it's the other way around: Economic security leads to*
> *better choices.* (62)

Upon this reflection of "devouring" in the ancient text and in the
present circumstance, you may want to ask, "Why have we never heard
any of these biblical texts in church? Why are they absent from the
lectionary, and from the horizon of the faith of the church?" Answers
to these questions will indicate some of the serious work we have to
do in the recovery of the claims of the gospel upon our common life.

❧ 3 ❧

LAZY

MY THIRD APPEAL to Desmond concerns his probe into the social labeling of "lazy." In his chapter on "welfare" in *Poverty, by America*, he calls attention to the insistent teaching of capitalism with an appeal to the harsh stricture of Joseph Townsend:

Perhaps it's because we've been trained since the earliest days of capitalism to see the poor as idle and unmotivated. The world's first capitalists faced a problem that titans of industry still face today: how to get the masses to file into their mills and slaughterhouses to work for as little pay as the law and market allow. Hunger was the capitalists' solution to the labor question. "The poor know little of the motives which stimulate the higher ranks to action—pride, honour, and ambition. In general it is only hunger which can spur and goad them on to labour." So wrote the English doctor and clergyman Joseph Townsend in his 1786 treatise, A Dissertation on the Poor Laws, By a Well-Wisher of Mankind, *asserting a position that would become common sense, then common law, throughout the early modern period. The "unremitted pressure" of hunger, Townsend continued, offered "the most natural motive to industry."*
(83–84)

Capitalism consistently faces the problem of how to motivate poorly paid and poorly treated workers to do the hard work on which production and wealth depend. The dismissive labeling of workers has repeatedly led to the conclusion that such workers can only be motivated by harsh measures that amount to rationing resources and thus coercing work from those perceived as unwilling. We may identify in Desmond's chapter, "How We Rely on Welfare," three facets of the dominant stereotypes of capitalist propaganda:

1. Desmond takes a good hard look at how well-off people view the poor. He reiterates, in critical fashion, the way in which the well-off *label the poor as "lazy."*

2. Desmond considers how the labeling of the poor as "lazy" has dominated thinking about welfare programs. He opines that it is the "protected class" that claims *the large share of "welfare payments,"* while the poor are very slow to sign on for their proper benefits.

> *The rest of us, on the other hand—we members of the*
> *protected classes—have grown increasingly dependent on*
> *our welfare programs. In 2020 the federal government*
> *spent more than $193 billion on homeowner subsidies,*
> *a figure that far exceeded the amount spent on direct*
> *housing assistance for low-income families ($53 billion).*
> *Most families who enjoy those subsidies have six-figure*
> *incomes and are white. Poor families lucky enough to live*
> *in government-owned apartments often have to deal with*
> *mold and even lead paint, while rich families are claiming*
> *mortgage interest deductions on first and second homes. The*

lifetime limit for cash welfare to poor parents is five years,
but families claiming the mortgage interest deduction may
do so for the length of the mortgage, typically thirty years. A
fifteen-story public housing tower and a mortgaged suburban
home are both government-subsidized, but only one looks
(and feels) that way. (90–91)

Desmond concludes:

We're all on the dole . . . Today, the biggest beneficiaries of
federal aid are affluent families. To benefit from employer-
sponsored health insurance, you need a good job, usually one
that requires a college degree. To benefit from the mortgage
interest deduction, you need to be able to afford a home, and
those who can afford the biggest mortgages reap the biggest
deductions. To benefit from a 529 plan, you need to be able
to squirrel away cash for your children's college costs, and
the more you save, the bigger your tax break, which is why
this subsidy is almost exclusively used by the well-off . . . The
American government gives the most help to those who need
it least. This is the true nature of our welfare state, and it has
far-reaching implications, not only for our bank accounts
and poverty levels, but also for our psychology and civic spirit.
(92, 93, 95)

3. Desmond does not spend much time on it, but sees how the destructive force of welfare arrangements is most often *filtered through the lens of racism*, so that Black people are most often and regularly labeled as "lazy":

Studies have consistently identified two long-standing beliefs
harbored by the American public. First, Americans tend to
believe (wrongly) that most welfare recipients are Black. This
is true for both liberals and conservatives. Second, many
Americans still believe Blacks have a low work ethic. . . .
The most recent iteration of the survey, conducted in 2021,
found that more than one in seven Americans still saw Black
Americans as lazy. Anti-Black racism hardens Americans'
antagonism toward social benefits. (86)

These three recurring factors in time result in the draconian
measures against the poor, either to dismiss their needs as "their own
fault," or to impose such penalizing requirements as work in order
to "earn" welfare income. Desmond shows us the way in which this
common misrepresentation of the poor has shaped policy, and how
relentless propaganda has sustained and reinforced such policies.

When we consider biblical texts concerning this distortion,
we find ample reinforcement for it in the teachings in Proverbs. The
sayings in Proverbs likely reflect the political discernment and interest
of small farmers in peasant communities who greatly prized a stable,
orderly economy that enjoyed no surplus wealth:

This community life has its ethical atmosphere; it compels
the individual to live up to specific expectations which people
have of him, it provides him with long-established examples
and values. As a rule, the individual conforms unthinkingly
to these community-determined factors; but, vice versa,
the rules of behavior are also, in turn, conformed to these
factors . . . Its ideas are characterized by a thoroughly static

quality. Its statements try to grasp life from the aspect of that
which always remains the same; they are open not to daily
social problems, but to that which is generally valid and
which survives no matter what the social circumstances . . .
This social order is regarded as given and is obviously stable.
At any rate, it is never itself the subject of discussion. It is
neither theologically justified nor subjected to radical criticism.
(Gerhard von Rad, *Wisdom in Israel,* 75, 76, 85)

The wisdom teaching was designed to reinforce and legitimate economic, communal stability with a simple cause-and-effect reasoning that served the interests of the peasant patriarchy. In such an over-simplified world of *cause and effect,* it was easy enough to see that poverty was caused by idleness and laziness, and refusal to do the work that preceded wealth. Thus, Proverbs teems with dismissive critiques of idleness:

A slack hand causes poverty,
but the hand of the diligent makes rich.
A child who gathers in summer is prudent,
but a child who sleeps in harvest brings shame. (10:4–5)

The appetite of the lazy craves and gets nothing,
while the appetite of the diligent is richly supplied. (13:4)

Laziness brings on deep sleep;
an idle person will suffer hunger. (19:15)

The lazy person does not plow in season;
harvest comes, and there is nothing to be found. (20:4)

Do not love sleep, or else you will come to poverty;
open your eyes, and you will have plenty of bread. (20:13)

The craving of the lazy person is fatal,
for lazy hands refuse to labor. (21:25)

I passed by the field of one who was lazy,
by the vineyard of a stupid person;
and see, it was all overgrown with thorns,
the ground was covered with nettles,
and its stone wall was broken down.
Then I saw and considered it;
I looked and received instruction.
A little sleep, a little slumber,
a little folding of the hands to rest,
and poverty will come upon you like a robber,
and want, like an armed warrior. (24:30–33; see Eccl 10:18)

These examples could be multiplied, as the wisdom teachers endlessly reiterated the requirement and expectation that sustained a viable social stability. Thus, Hans Walter Wolff, *Anthropology of the Old Testament*, has reviewed all this material. His discussion of work, however, ends with an important caveat (pp.131–132). In the end, the reliable *quid pro quo* of such work and wealth is interrupted by the recognition that it is finally the wonder of God's blessing (not human effort) that gives wealth and well-being. Wolff concludes:

Thus Israel's wisdom teaches a right understanding of work.
Man has to accept the rules; but above all he has to recognize

the Lord of the rules. Then he will be kept from falling lower
than the animals (the ant, for example!) through his laziness;
or from usurping the place of God in his self-deception. (133)

The balance of Wolff's final statements is worth notice. Disregard of
the governance of God may lead to *laziness*; right! But that same disregard may lead to *"self-deception,"* a temptation among the well-off to
imagine themselves to be self-made, and so entitled to a Promethean
self-assertion. The reality of God trespasses the confidence in a quid pro
quo calculation and renders such reasoning to be penultimate. While
these qualifications are of immense importance, they are evidently not
enough to lower the tone of self-assurance of those who confidently
accept the harsh rule of quid pro quo.

The affirmation of Yahweh's rule, however, opens the way for us
to consider a very different example of work and laziness in Scripture,
namely the Exodus narrative. That narrative is recited at Passover time
as a recall of Egyptian oppression and Hebrew enslavement. It does
not matter what "historical" judgment we make about the narrative,
because it functions in a paradigmatic way in Israel's practice. Thus, the
narrative pertains to any and every historical circumstance over time
wherein the power-class imposes its tireless, inexhaustible demand on
a labor force that is vulnerable and powerless in the face of coercion.

In that paradigmatic recital, "Pharaoh" represents the uncompromising ownership-class that relies on cheap labor as the source
of its wealth and well-being. Thus, in the narrative Pharaoh's aim is
the construction of granaries (storehouse cities) to store his surplus
wealth in the form of grain. (See James C. Scott, *Against the Grain:*
A Deep History of the Earliest States, 2017.) Pharaoh has no interest
in or connection to his cheap labor force, but only insists upon the

endless construction of bricks for granary storage. But the narrative is told "from below," from the perspective of the exploited work force. That exploited labor force, without much imagination, readily recites Pharaoh's work expectation that I have elsewhere labeled "Pharaoh's Ten Commandments." In Exodus 5, we can trace out ten such requirements, but all of them amount to a demand for greater production.

Exodus 5 amounts to a critical exposé of the reasoning of Pharaoh that revolves around the indictment of his cheap labor force by Pharaoh:

> But you shall require of them the same quantity of bricks as they have made previously; do not diminish it, for they are lazy. (Exod 5:8)

> You are lazy, lazy; that is why you say, "Let us go and sacrifice to the Lord." (5:17)

Thus, Pharaoh is an anticipation of our later dismissive labeling of the poor as "lazy." That verdict is reached by a simple appeal to a quid pro quo calculus read backward. Read forward, one can see that the labor force has ended in desperation and poverty. When the calculus is reversed, it is no wonder that their desperation and poverty are caused by laziness. There is, however, no evidence in the narrative that the Hebrew slaves are lazy. They kept getting larger and larger brick quotas, not unlike the cotton quotas of Black slaves in the US as the English needed more cotton for their mills.

It is worth seeing the tension in the Bible between the *assured teaching of wisdom* concerning laziness (idleness), and the *function of "laziness" as a dismissive label* in the propaganda of Pharaoh, used both to legitimate endless production, and to diminish the dignity and viability of the slave population.

I have no doubt that the tension between "laziness" in Proverbs and "laziness" in Exodus is a tension worth noticing in the church in a maximum way. It is a common assumption that the Bible speaks in one voice. It does not. It speaks in many voices, each of which reflects a certain dimension of social reality. The voice that speaks in Proverbs is a voice "*from above*," from a patriarchal perspective that aims to impose and sustain its order of property and well-being. The voice that sounds in Exodus is "*from below*," reflecting the needs, pain, and desperation of those who are left bereft in a socioeconomic arrangement of predation.

It is an endless temptation to read the Bible according to our vested interests. That is a longstanding practice of the well-off church. In such a church that reads and lives "from above," the calculus of Proverbs is persuasive. But of course the gospel does not permit us to read the Bible simply as an echo of our vested interests. The gospel invites (requires!) us to read outside of our comfort zone of vested interest in the interest of "justice and righteousness." And when we do that, we may indeed read from an angle of vision other than our own. Thus, we are invited to see how the narrative of Exodus 5, for example, speaks out against our comfort zone in Proverbs. Given the angle of vision of that chapter, we may again ask of Exodus 5, "Who is speaking here?" Well, it is exactly the slave community that knows precisely what Pharaoh thinks, and how Pharaoh can readily justify enslavement. But then, remembering that the narrative is paradigmatic and not a one-off report, we may press further the question, "Who is speaking here?" to see that the narrative is the voice of *all those on the underside of the economy who must endlessly produce too little gain for themselves.* And whatever they produce, it is not enough. It is never enough! It will always yield an easy verdict, lazy, idle, unproductive, irresponsible, uncaring, etc.

The biblical narrative, however, tells the contrary. It tells that God noticed the suffering of the slaves (Exod 2:23–25). God saw the affliction! God heard the groans! God acted to overthrow such a system of exploitation. And then at Sinai, God authorized an *alternative economy*. Thus, the Ten Commandments are intended exactly as a form of resistance against Pharaoh's exploitative system of production (Exod 20:1–17). At the center of the "Big Ten" is provision for *Sabbath rest* from work (Exod 20:8–11). At the conclusion of the "Big Ten" is a prohibition against coveting (Exod 20:17). This is "a more excellent way," but it is a way made possible only by a clear discernment of how present predatory practice and policy traffic in exploitation, all the while justified by the demeaning labeling of the poor. The church can only ask its members to host the tension and to be informed by that tension. It is a tension between *convenient self-deception* and an *inconvenient truth*. As Desmond shows, poverty is not the result of laziness. It is the outcome of an economy that is designed to sustain an illusion:

> *Do we really believe the top 1 percent are more deserving*
> *than the rest of the country? Are we really, in 2023, going*
> *to argue that white people have far more wealth than Black*
> *people because white people have worked harder for it—or*
> *that women are paid less because they deserve less? Do we*
> *have the audacity to point to housekeepers with skin peeling*
> *from chemicals or berry pickers who can no longer stand up*
> *straight or the millions of other poor working Americans and*

claim that they are stuck at the bottom because they are lazy?
(99–100)

Desmond finishes with the simple, honest justification of the illusion:

Those who are well-heeled don't want to get un-well-healed.
(101)

    I will finish with a Bible verse not often read among us. In his allegory, Ezekiel has likened Judah to "Sodom." Of course, the popular notion is that "Sodom" concerns homosexuality. Ezekiel, however, has a very different notion of the sin of Sodom (Judah):

This was the guilt of your sister Sodom: she and her daughters
had pride, excess of food, and prosperous ease, but did not aid
the poor and needy. (Ezek 16:49)

It is not sex! It is economics! The well-off of the Jerusalem elites are marked by luxurious pride, extravagant food, and self-indulgent ease. They are indeed, "at ease in Zion" (Amos 6:1). Being at ease blinded them to the coming trouble of a dysfunctional economy. They refused to see the coming trouble. Their ease functions like a narcotic against noticing. Pharaoh is an epitome of such indifference that is covered over by the slogans of race and class. The narrative of Exodus 5 is a mighty summons against the illusion. It is a narrative that continues in many other venues, not least in the tale of Jesus of Nazareth. Those who notice and care do not sign on for convenient self-deception, the kind that Wolff says, "usurps the place of God."

PRIVATE OPULENCE AND PUBLIC SQUALOR

MY FOURTH APPEAL to Desmond concerns his articulation of the great economic crisis between "haves" and "have-nots" in our society that he labels "private opulence and public squalor." Desmond utilizes this critical phrase five times in *Poverty, by America*:

> *What happens to a country when fortunes diverge so sharply,*
> *when millions of poor people live alongside millions of rich ones?*
> *In a country with such vast inequality, the poor increasingly*
> *come to depend on public services and the rich increasingly*
> *seek to divest from them. This leads to* "private opulence and
> public squalor," *a self-reinforcing dynamic that transforms our*
> *communities in ways that pull us further apart.* (105)

> *Extreme displays of* private opulence and public squalor *are*
> *seen throughout the sprawling buzzing cities of the developing*
> *world.* (106)

> *Follow the money, all of it, and you can see how a trend toward*
> private opulence and public squalor *has come to define not*
> *simply a handful of communities, but the whole nation . . . Tax*
> *cuts are one of the main engines of* private opulence and

public squalor, *and in recent decades we have grown used to the Republican Party delivering them.* (107, 109)

The drive toward private opulence and public squalor harms the poor not only because it leads to widespread disinvestment in public goods but also because that disinvestment creates new private enterprises that eventually replace public institutions as the primary suppliers of opportunity. As more affluent citizens come to rely on those private enterprises, they withdraw their support from public institutions even more. In this way, divestment from public goods does not spur renewed attention or motivate reinvestment; it brings further disinvestment and, at the extreme, energizes calls to privatize even our most treasured public institutions such as the U. S. Postal Service and popular programs like Social Security. (111)

Desmond regards tax cuts as a major cause of the gross income and wealth differential among us. Tax cuts for the rich move money away from the common good toward private indulgence. Thus, the surge toward privatization continues to cause disinvestment in the common good and from widely needed shared public resources. One outcome of such disinvestment is commoditization in which what is needed for a viable life is "for sale" for those who can afford to buy it, and deprivation for those who cannot afford to pay for it. Such a growing gap between haves and have-nots marks the advancement of the indices of poverty.

This contemporary reality of the gap is evident in Scripture. We may take the portrayal of the self-indulgent King Solomon as a case in point. In 1 Kings 10 we have a narrative in which the Queen of Sheba is dazzled by the king's opulence to which she willingly contributes:

> *Then she gave the king one hundred twenty talents of gold, a*
> *great quantity of spices, and precious stones; never again did*
> *spices come in such quantity as that which the queen of Sheba*
> *gave to King Solomon.* (1 Kings 10:10)

This is a portrayal of limitless luxury continued in the remainder of the chapter. In verse 8, moreover, we have this careful phrasing:

> *Happy are your wives! Happy are these your servants, who*
> *continually attend you and hear your wisdom!* (v. 8)

The two "happy" populations are those close to the royal circle, his wives (700 princesses and 300 concubines!), and his "servants." The latter refers to the oligarchs of priests, scribes, and counselors who engaged the king's company. It was a small circle that enjoyed the king's opulence. Contrasted is the great peasant population that elsewhere in Solomon's narrative are (a) reduced to serfdom or slavery (1 Kgs 5:13–16), and (b) participated in tax revolt because of the impositions of the state (1 Kgs12:1–19). While Desmond's "squalor" may be too much for this population, it is easy to see that the peasants lived a quite disadvantaged life and were at the mercy of the usurpative propensity of the state. Solomon was a practitioner of great opulence that in turn produced public resentment in the extreme.

This state of affairs between haves and have-nots produced by privatization and the withdrawal of wealth from the common good is a major subject of the prophetic tradition of Israel, especially expressed through the pattern of a rhetorical "lawsuit" of indictment and sentence. The model prophetic "lawsuit" in Hosea 4:1–3 is noticeably terse.

Indictment:

> *There is no faithfulness or loyalty, and no knowledge of God*
> *in the land.*
> *Swearing, lying, and murder,*
> *and stealing and adultery break out;*
> *bloodshed follows bloodshed.* (Hos 4:1–2)

Sentence:

> *Therefore the land mourns,*
> *and all who live in it languish;*
> *together with the wild animals and the birds of the air,*
> *even the fish of the sea are perishing.* (v. 3)

The prophet refers to a lack of public fidelity and solidarity. Such a state of affairs, he insists, produces drought and the shriveling of the economy. In large sweep, the prophets affirm that economic disparity produces a profound environmental crisis. In general, the prophets do not propose a remedy to this deeply-based economic crisis. They suggest that the wealthy must reverse course and invest in the common good for the sake of the well-being of the whole.

Among the fullest presentations of private opulence is the oracle of Amos:

> *Alas for those who lie on beds of ivory,*
> *and lounge on their couches,*

and eat lambs from the flock,
and calves from the stall;
who sing idle songs to the sound of the harp,
and like David improvise on instruments of music;
who drink wine from bowls, and anoint themselves
with the finest oils . . . (Amos 6:4–6a)

The oracle begins with "alas," that we may take to mean, "big trouble coming." Big trouble is coming from God when private opulence diminishes a communal economy. Thus, the prophet details the causes of such an "alas." His words linger over the imagery of self-indulgence:

- beds of ivory . . . while subsistence farmers sleep on straw
- lambs . . . while subsistence farmers have to let sheep grow for mutton
- calves . . . while subsistence farmers have to grow calves into cows
- idle songs . . . leisure time for inane, perhaps boring amusement
- drink from bowls . . . gulped, not sipped, in large quantities

Valuable commodities used daily with careless indifference. The scene is one of extreme wealth, comfort, and self-indulgence. The climax of the prophetic indictment, however, is in the words that follow:

but are not grieved over the ruin of Joseph! (v. 6b)

They do not notice that society is going to hell in a handbasket. How could they notice? Their vision is skewed by indulgence. Their discernment is hampered by excessive well-being. It is inevitable, in prophetic horizon, that the "therefore" of judgment must follow in verse 7 with a scathing anticipation of exile:

> *Therefore they shall now be the first to go into exile,*
> *and the revelry of the loungers shall pass away.* (Amos 6:7)

The displacement will negate their extravagances. The prophets judge that in a world of moral coherence the widening gap of opulence and squalor is unsustainable, even if it comes as a surprise to those who should have known better. The counterpoint to such opulence is voiced in Amos 8:4–6 that characterizes the ways in which the greedy trick the vulnerable poor. They are endlessly exploitative . . . , greedy Sabbath imagery, rigged scales, and cheap labor.

The prophet Isaiah offers a scene of limitless indulgence among the women of Jerusalem, "daughters of Zion":

> *Because the daughters of Zion are haughty*
> *and walk with outstretched necks,*
> *glancing wantonly with their eyes*
> *mincing along as they go,*
> *tinkling with their feet.* (Isa 3:16)

In a mocking tone, Isaiah catalogs their luxurious clothes closets that overflow with indulgence:

> *In that day the Lord will take away the finery of the anklets,*
> *the headbands, and the crescents; the pendants, the bracelets,*
> *and the scarfs; the headdresses, the armlets, the sashes, the*

perfume boxes, and the amulets; the signet rings and nose
rings; the festal robes, the mantles, the cloaks, and the
handbags; the garments of gauze, the linen garments, the
turbans, and the veils. (vv. 18–23)

And then abruptly:

Instead,
    Instead,
        Instead,
            Instead!
                Instead. Five times!

The conclusion can only be "lament and mourn" the loss (v. 26).

Jeremiah adds his rhetoric to this sad scenario of an economy failed in indifference. On the one hand:

They have become great and rich,
they have grown fat and sleek. (Jer 5:27–28)

They eat too well and that rich food evokes indifference. On the other hand, an abundance of public squalor:

They do not judge with justice the cause of the orphan, to make
    it prosper,
and they do not defend the rights of the needy. (v. 28)

The elite in Jerusalem are so self-preoccupied that they do not notice the vulnerable public. Their appetites have devoured what may have been a social safety net . . . of food stamps, or health care provision, or housing subsidies. It is all eaten up by opulence!

Finally in a portrayal of such private opulence, the prophet Ezekiel details the goods on offer in commercial transactions. The inventory is assigned to the commerce of Tyre, but "Tyre" is simply a placeholder for every society that has reduced all relationships to commodity transactions. Here is the list:

> *Tarshish did business with you out of the abundance of your*
> *great wealth; silver, iron, tin, and lead they exchanged for*
> *your wares. Javan, Tubal, and Meshech traded with you;*
> *they exchanged* human beings *and vessels of bronze for your*
> *merchandise. Bethtogarmah exchanged for your wares horses,*
> *war horses, and mules. The Rhodians traded with you; many*
> *coastlands were your own special markets; they brought you*
> *in payment ivory tusks and ebony. Edom did business with*
> *you because of your abundant goods; they exchanged for your*
> *wares turquoise, purple, embroidered work, fine linen, coral,*
> *and rubies. Judah and the land of Israel traded with you;*
> *they exchanged for your merchandise wheat from Minnith,*
> *millet, honey, oil, and balm. Damascus traded with you for*
> *your abundant goods—because of your great wealth of every*
> *kind—wine of Helbon, and white wool. Vedan and Javan*
> *from Uzal entered into trade for your wares; wrought iron,*
> *cassia, and sweet cane were bartered for your merchandise.*
> *Dedan traded with you in saddlecloths for riding. Arabia*
> *and all the princes of Kedar were your favored dealers in*
> *lambs, rams, and goats; in these they did business with you.*
> *The merchants of Sheba and Raamah traded with you; they*

exchanged for your wares the best of all kinds of spices, and
all precious stones, and gold. Haran, Canneh, Eden, the
merchants of Sheba, Asshur, and Chilmad traded with you.
These traded with you in choice garments, in clothes of blue
and embroidered work, and in carpets of colored material,
bound with cords and made secure; in these they traded with
you. The ships of Tarshish traveled for you in your trade.
(Ezek 27:12–25)

I take time to reiterate the entire inventory (as does Ezekiel), so
that we may pause, item by item, to notice the exotic nature of the
goods on offer. We may ask of such goods, who needs them? Or
what are they good for? The answer of course is that they are only
"needed" by the utterly self-indulgent who have too much money
and too much time on their hands. And the reason they have too
much money is that they do not adequately contribute, via taxation, to the common good—so Desmond. We may consider how
these commercial goods looked and sounded to the subsistence
peons who could just get by on their meager income as they paid
their tax burden.

It is important to notice that in verse 13 "human beings" are
listed along with the commercial goods. When everything is reduced to
a commodity, so also human persons can be bought and sold, perhaps
as a cheap labor force, perhaps as sex traffic. Either way, the humanity
of such "commodity" is forgotten and disregarded. Such persons have
no rights and surely no access to economic support for housing, health,
or education. (Notice in Revelation 18:11–13 we have an abbreviated
reiteration of the list as pertains to the Roman Empire, the last entry
providing "slaves—and human lives"! It is the way of every economy in

which policymakers are smitten with self-indulgence that other more
vulnerable human persons are reduced to a supply for a devouring
appetite.

Desmond is unflinching in his analysis of the situation in the US
economy. He includes all shades of politics in his indictment:

> *Progressive cities have built the highest walls, passing a*
> *tangle of exclusionary zoning policies . . . Most Americans*
> *want the country to build more public housing for*
> *low-income families, but they do not want that public*
> *housing (or any sort of multifamily housing) in their*
> *neighborhood. Democrats are more likely than Republicans*
> *to champion public housing in the abstract, but among*
> *homeowners, they are no more likely to welcome new*
> *housing developments in their own backyards . . . If you*
> *erect a community of expensive, beautiful homes and prop*
> *up the value of those homes by making it illegal to build*
> *more housing, which turns your home into a resource so*
> *scarce that potential buyers do things like writing pleading*
> *letters or make cash offers above the asking price or bid*
> *sight unseen—behavior that has become commonplace in*
> *liberal cities like Austin, Seattle, and Cambridge—then*
> *you pretty much want to keep things as they are. If you*
> *design a public school system such that it primarily serves*
> *students of professional parents, who have the time and*
> *know-how to invest in their children's schooling, and who*
> *can afford to pay for extra tutoring and college prep coaches*
> *and out-of-state field trips and therapy, you can create an*

enriching educational environment and pipeline to college.
(115, 117)

Indeed, Desmond goes on to notice, among others, the message of candidate Joe Biden:

> *When then-presidential-candidate Joe Biden told a room of*
> *wealthy donors that "nothing would fundamentally change"*
> *if he were to be elected, he was repeating a familiar liberal*
> *talking point:* If you join me in this effort to reduce
> inequality you yourself benefit from, you won't have to
> give up a thing. *These "everybody wins" arguments ring false*
> *because they are.* (118)

Desmond ends with a note of honesty about a remedy:

> *Let's be honest. Sharing opportunities previously hoarded*
> *doesn't mean everyone wins. It means that those who have*
> *benefitted from the nation's excesses will have to take less so*
> *that others may share in the bounty.* (118)

He insists, nevertheless, that a remedy can be enacted, on terms that are "irresistibly attainable" (125):

> *I'm not calling for "redistribution." I'm calling for the rich*
> *to pay their taxes. I'm calling for a rebalancing of our social*
> *safety net. I'm calling for a return to a time when America*
> *made bigger investments in the general welfare. I'm calling*

for more poor aid and less rich aid . . . We need to empower
the poor. (132, 138)

Some will dismiss such investment as "socialism." But it is not; and the church has no particular stake in "socialism." Rather, the church has a stake in our common life, and thus in the maintenance and protection of the "commons." It is the good work of the church to champion the urgency of the commons which, among other things, means funding via taxation of the essentials for a good life, including adequate housing, health care, and education. It may seem odd to say the church should champion such taxation, but I have no doubt that as the church teaches responsibility concerning "stewardship," the funding of the common good via taxation is part of responsible stewardship. Conversely, the church must voice its resistance to the devastation of the commons in the interest of private security and, eventually, opulence.

So here are three biblical narratives concerning the withholding of wealth from the common good:

1. The crude primitive story of Achan in Joshua 7. In the narrative Israel has lost a decisive battle. Joshua learns that the defeat is because someone in Israel has withheld goods from the common fund for their own private passion:

> *Israel has sinned; they have transgressed my covenant that I*
> *imposed on them. They have taken some of the devoted things;*
> *they have stolen, they have acted deceitfully, and they have*
> *put them among their own belongings.* (Josh 7:11)

Upon systematic investigation, Achan confesses to the sin:

> *I am the one who sinned against the Lord God of Israel. This*
> *is what I did: when I saw among the spoil a beautiful mantle*
> *from Shinar, and two hundred shekels of silver, and a bar*
> *of gold weighing fifty shekels, then I coveted them and took*
> *them.* (vv. 20–21)

Achan details the beauty of the objects taken and admits coveting enough to withhold from the common treasury. His "coveting" brought trouble enough that the place is called, "The Valley of Trouble" (v. 26). It is always "trouble" enough when withholding from the common good is practiced.

2. In the narrative of the early church it is reported that the people of the community held "all things in common" (Acts 2:44). They lived "with glad and generous hearts" (v. 46). In a subsequent note Joseph the Cypriot,

> *sold a field that belonged to him, then brought the money,*
> *and laid it at the apostles' feet.* (Acts 4:37)

Then, immediately, we get the story of Ananias and Sapphire, members of the community, who held back from the church profit from a sale of property (Act 5:1–11). In time, both died from their "lie to God," as they held back from the common good.

3. In the parable of Luke 16:19–31, Jesus features a nameless "rich man" and a "poor man" named Lazarus. The parable lines out the destiny of both of them. The rich man gets the place of torment; the poor man lands in the embrace of the bosom of Father Abraham.

The parable ends without comment, but clearly the investment in or withholding from the common good would create futures for one's self. The management of our resources vis-à-vis the community matters ultimately in the governance of God.

Finally, here is a folksier commentary. In a congregation where I once belonged, we had a more-or-less regular potluck dinner to which members brought their food for the common table. One aging (quite moneyed) couple regularly brought a special dessert. They did not put it on the common table but held it back for their own table for their specially selected friends. There is no report that this "withholding" created any special future, but it makes one wonder. The recurring episode reminds me of the small crisis concerning the Lord's Table in 1 Corinthians 11:17–22. As Desmond sees so clearly, a great deal is at stake in the withholding from the common good. This will not be resolved among us until we who have so much see as our proper work the finding of the commons for the sake of all of us, including widows, orphans, and immigrants. Public life costs, but we cannot live without it. Privatization will not provide what we need for our common well-being.

✖ 5 ✖

SCARCITY-CUM-SEGREGATION

MY FIFTH APPEAL to Desmond concerns his exposition of "scarcity" in chapter 9 of *Poverty, by America*. He wonders,

> *Why do we continue to accept scarcity as given, treating it as the central organizing principle of our economics, policy-making, city planning, and personal ethics?* (175)

He offers a wondrous articulation of what he terms "the scarcity diversion," that is, a focus on scarcity as a diversion from addressing real problems with real solutions:

> *Here's the playbook. First, allow elites to hoard a resource like money or land. Second, pretend that arrangement is natural, unavoidable—or better yet, ignore it altogether. Third, attempt to address social problems caused by the resource hoarding with only the scarce resources left over. So instead of making the rich pay all their taxes, for instance, design a welfare state around the paltry budget you are left with when they don't. Fourth, fail. Fail to drive down the poverty rate. Fail to build more affordable housing. Fifth, claim this is the best we can do. Preface your comments by saying, "In a world of scarce resources . . ." Blame government programs. Blame capitalism. Blame the other political party. Blame*

> *immigrants. Blame anyone you can except those who most*
> *deserve it. "Gaslighting" is not too strong a phrase to describe*
> *such pretense.* (174–175)

The trick is in the second element, to treat "scarcity" as "natural" and "unavoidable." Once scarcity is accepted as a socioeconomic reality, there surely will follow an absence of will and action to solve issues effectively because "there is not enough, in any case, to go around."

The response to an acceptance of "scarcity" as a socioeconomic reality is what Desmond terms "segregation," the erection of barriers to separate those who have access from those who are denied access. Thus, a fear of scarcity leads to policies designed to have the effect of division and discrimination between haves and have-nots.

Segregation may take various forms including racism. Thus, non-whites in our society have been systemically and consistently denied access to good schools, good housing, and good jobs, because such schools, housing, and jobs must be kept for those who have "legitimate" access to such opportunities. Thus, for example, Black veterans of World War II were regularly denied access to government funding through post-war grants to GIs for education. Over time our nation has gone through many torturous exercises to sort out the gradations and complexities of racist identity. But as Desmond sees, segregation is not only racist. There can also be "income segregation" so that school districts are readily compartmentalized to protect the affluent, and zoning ordinances are put in place to protect neighborhoods for the privileged, and roads are constructed across less favored communities:

> *Defenders of the status quo, this pro-segregationist propertied*
> *class, have shown themselves to be willing to do the tedious*

work of defending the wall. Their efforts have paid off in
terms of delaying and killing proposals to build more housing,
as local civil servants tend to respond to the voices they hear.
(169)

Desmond rightly sees that the compelling and essential response to an
ideology of scarcity that legitimates segregation is a "recognition of the
nation's bounty":

> *The ecologist Robin Wall Kimmerer has recently advocated*
> *for "an economy of abundance." Choosing abundance, at*
> *once a perspective and a legislative platform, a shift in vision*
> *and in policy design, means recognizing that this country*
> *has a profusion of resources—enough land and capital to go*
> *around—and that pretending otherwise is a farce. "I want*
> *to be part of a system in which wealth means having enough*
> *to share," Kimmerer writes, "and where the gratification of*
> *meeting your family needs is not poisoned by destroying that*
> *possibility for someone else" . . . Have we forgotten that there*
> *was a time, as E. P. Thompson has shown, when people found*
> *it immoral, even unnatural, to "profit from the necessities*
> *of others" even during seasons of drought and famine, and*
> *instead held up a "moral economy of provision"?* (175)

It turns out that "scarcity" and "abundance" are not simply labels
of economic reality. They are, rather, lenses through which we expe-
rience socioeconomic reality that strongly shapes our economy and
our way of life in the world. I have articulated the matter in an article
entitled, "The Liturgy of Abundance and the Myth of Scarcity" in

The Christian Century (March 24–31, 1999). In the article I took the term "liturgy" to refer to the continuing and unrestrained act of *public imagination* in the community where the lens of abundance was fully embraced. In that life-world, it was the lens through which its members could live the reality of abundance. In ancient Israel that "liturgy of abundance" was voiced in the creation narratives, and the great doxologies of the book of Psalms affirmed the creator God as the source of material abundance. Conversely, the "myth of scarcity" was a claim given through a phony lens generated by the powerful and affluent to justify their accumulation and monopoly of the food and life resources of creation. In this biblical juxtaposition, "abundance" is taken as the truth grounded in the reality of God, whereas "scarcity" is a false claim that contradicts the reality of the abundance-giving God. The weight of "true" and "false" in the Bible is tilted by the claim made for God. In other contexts without appeal to the claim for God, the matter can and will be differently adjudicated. Thus, we can see the contrast of abundance and scarcity, so clearly articulated by Desmond, as a primary issue of biblical faith. In the narrative imagination of Israel, Pharaoh is the great proponent of scarcity. His response to famine when there is to be a shortage of food (bread) was to secure for himself a monopoly of grain, and so to exercise inordinate power over vulnerable peasants. One result was that the Hebrew slaves in Egypt were preoccupied with constructing "storehouse cities" for Pharaoh's grain monopoly (Exod 1:11). James C. Scott, *Against the Grain: A Deep History of the Earliest States*, has shown that the earliest kingdoms and empires were made possible by the discovery that grain is a storable food commodity; grain could be accumulated and deployed as an instrument of power to leverage the economy in times of crisis. In the narrative of Genesis 47:13–26, Pharaoh's policy is one of accumulation of grain as a means of power to be used over and against vulnerable peasants. Pharaoh's policy served to enhance the claim of "scarcity." This Pharaoh is the same Pharaoh who enforced the habit that,

> *Egyptians could not eat with the Hebrews, for that is an abomination to the Egyptians.* (Gen 43:32)

We may imagine that Pharaoh had posted signs in every diner in Egypt, "We reserve the right to refuse service to any Hebrew." Thus, *segregation* goes along with *economic exploitation*. There was not enough grain to go around, and so the vulnerable had to rely on Pharaoh for life sustenance. Pharaoh in the biblical narrative is the model accumulator. It is fair to see that in ancient Israel his son-in-law, Solomon, practiced the same policy of accumulation and monopoly (1 Kgs 10). The matter is compellingly echoed in the teaching of Jesus in his parable concerning the "rich man" who produced abundance:

> *The land of a rich man produced abundantly. And he thought to himself, "What should I do, for I have no place to store my crops?" Then he said, "I will do this; I will pull down my barns and build larger ones, and there I will store all my grain and my goods."* (Luke 12:16–18)

The rich man in the parable, not unlike Pharaoh and Solomon, thought he could secure himself through his accumulation and monopoly. So in Desmond's narrative imagination, the walls of segregation, erected through redlining and zoning, aim to create and secure an environment of abundance for the affluent and a safe future for their privileged children. It is the insistence of biblical faith, right from the Exodus

narrative, that in a world governed by the creator God, such accumulation and monopoly are unsustainable in the long run. The practice of
accumulation and monopoly will never produce the hoped-for world
beyond fear and threat.

In the narrative of ancient Israel, the counter-theme to Pharaoh's
life-destroying monopoly is the wilderness narrative, a zone of reality
to which the governance of Pharaoh did not extend. It was readily
thought, even by the Hebrew slaves, that it was Pharaoh who generated their food supply. Their entry into the wilderness was entry into
a zone of extreme food urgency. By the second verse of entry into the
wilderness, Israel was beset by worry about food:

> *The whole congregation of the Israelites complained against*
> *Moses and Aaron in the wilderness. The Israelites said to*
> *them, "If only we had died by the hand of the Lord in the*
> *land of Egypt, when we sat by the fleshpots and ate our fill of*
> *bread; for you have brought us out into this wilderness to kill*
> *this whole assembly with hunger." (Exod 16:2–3).*

Their new circumstance evoked their bitter complaint, dispute, and
quarreling. What follows in Exodus 16, however, is one of the great
food episodes in the history of the world. It turns out, quite inexplicably, that the wilderness that seemed food-deprived became the venue
for "wonder bread" that was beyond Israel's expectation or explanation:

> *In the evening quails came up and covered the camp, and*
> *in the morning there was a layer of dew around the camp.*
> *When the layer of dew lifted, there on the surface of the*
> *wilderness was a fine flaky substance, as fine as frost on the*

ground. When the Israelites saw it, they said to one another,
"What is it?" For they did not know what it was. Moses said
to them, "It is the bread that the Lord has given you to eat."
(Exod 16:13–15)

They received meat and bread that they could not explain. In the next
chapter, moreover, the wilderness as a place of "no water," became
again inexplicably, a place of water (Exod 17:1–7). It is the high drama
of the Bible to juxtapose Egypt and wilderness as respectively a place
of *predatory monopoly* and a place of *inexplicable generosity*. The narrative is staged so that Israel is always required to choose between the
scarcity propelled by Pharaoh and *abundance* given by the creator God.
It is no different in Desmond's analysis wherein scarcity dominates so
much of our common life, and Desmond's compelling advocacy for a
counter-action:

Lift the floor by rebalancing our social safety net; empower
the poor by reining in exploitation; and invest in broad
prosperity by turning away from segregation. That's how we
end poverty in America. (176)

The claim of abundance in ancient Israel is endlessly reiterated in
the great liturgies and doxologies of abundance in the book of Psalms.
The singing of doxology—loud and unrestrained—is itself an exercise
in abundance that defies the fearful ideology of scarcity and that maps
out a world where generosity is appropriate:

You cause the grass to grow for the cattle,
and plants for people to use,

> *to bring forth food from the earth,*
> *and wine to gladden the human heart,*
> *oil to make the face shine,*
> *and bread to strengthen the human heart.* (Ps 104:14–15)

The wilderness wonder is explicitly reiterated in doxology:

> *They asked, and he brought quails,*
> *And he gave them food from heaven in abundance.*
> *He opened the rock, and water gushed out;*
> *it flowed through the desert like a river.* (Ps 105:40–41)

From such specificity Israel can readily generalize in its singing:

> *He turns rivers into a desert,*
> *springs of water into thirsty ground,*
> *a fruitful land into a salty waste,*
> *because of the wickedness of its inhabitants.*
> *He turns a desert into pools of water,*
> *a parched land into springs of water.*
> *And there he lets the hungry live,*
> *and they establish a town to live in;*
> *they sow fields, and plant vineyards,*
> *and get a fruitful yield.* (Ps 107:33–37)

> *You visit the earth and water it,*
> *you greatly enrich it;*
> *the river of God is full of water;*

you provide the people with grain,
for so you have prepared it.
You water its furrows abundantly,
settling its ridges,
softening it with showers,
and blessing its growth.
You crown the year with your bounty;
your wagon tracks overflow with richness.
The pastures of the wilderness overflow,
the hills gird themselves with joy,
the meadows clothe themselves with flocks,
the valleys deck themselves with grain,
they shout and sing together for joy. (Ps 65:9–13)

Such abundance leaves Israel awed in gratitude:

The eyes of all look to you,
and you give them their food in due season.
You open your hand,
satisfying the desire of every living thing. (Ps 145:15–16)

Happy are those whose help is the God of Jacob,
whose hope is in the Lord their God,
who made heaven and earth,
the sea, and all that is in them;
who keeps faith forever;
who executes justice for the oppressed;
who gives food to the hungry. (Ps 146:5–7)

He gives to the animals their food,
and to the young ravens when they cry.
His delight is not in the strength of horses,
nor his pleasure in the speed of a runner;
but the Lord takes pleasure in those who fear him,
in those who hope in his steadfast love . . .
He grants peace within your borders;
he fills you with the finest of wheat. (Ps 147:9–14)

Eventually Israel's awe and praise is so extravagant that it need no longer express specificity, but dissolves into doxological wonder that yields all of life back to God in praise. Such a doxological tradition cannot and will not linger in *safety*, but will come to expression in *generosity* that zones out none who need a share.

This testimony to God-given abundance is extended in and through the life of Jesus in his food narrative. Not unlike Israel, Jesus and the crowd with him are in a wilderness place (Mark 6:32). Not unlike Israel, the crowd is hungry. And not unlike God in "the murmur tradition," Jesus responds to the hunger of the crowd and inexplicably provides food (Mark 6:41–44). His wondrous action is a defiance of the entire security system of Rome and official Judaism. The action and outcome of the narrative is that Jesus, not unlike God in the wilderness, exposes the myth of scarcity as a ruse designed to protect exploitative monopoly.

Israel, in its great fear, did its best to "segregate." Over time its sacerdotal leadership devised rules and categories of "clean and unclean" to determine who was in and who was out, who had access to the goodies of life and who was disqualified. As the Holiness Code of Leviticus and the catalog of Deuteronomy 14 indicate, there is no end to the detail and refinement of the laws of exclusion, a refinement that has been belatedly reiterated in the complex laws of racial identification in and through US history.

Such rule-based exclusion—rules characteristically devised by the powerful and affluent—never went without challenge in ancient Israel. Thus, in the face of "holiness," the tradition of Deuteronomy very differently voices a concern for civic justice that was measured by need and not by qualification. This counter-theme in the Torah and its rhetorical tradition reaches something of a climax in the anticipation of Isaiah 56. Against the exclusions of the temple that segregated according to the "Holy of Holies," "the holy place," and the "outer court" (see 1 Kgs 6), this prophetic anticipation affirms:

> *These [foreigners and eunuchs] I will bring to my holy*
> > *mountain,*
> *and make them joyful in my house of prayer;*
> *their burnt offerings and their sacrifices*
> *will be accepted on my altar;*
> *for my house shall be called a house of prayer for all peoples.*
> (Isa 56:7)

Included among the welcome invitees are "foreigners" (v. 3) and "eunuchs" (v. 4). It is suggested, for example, that the inclusion of foreigners and eunuchs is intended as a positive counterpoint to, and refutation of, the exclusionary provisions of Deuteronomy 23:1–8. That text pertains to those with "crushed testicles" and foreigners. The intent of the prophet is that the fear-based exclusions of ancient time will not and cannot pertain amid the generous offer of God's extravagant inclusiveness. Thus, the contradiction between claims of fearful exclusion and generous inclusion is endlessly reperformed. Now, among us, we are facing a vigorous reassertion of fearful exclusion as concerns variously people of color, LGBTQ people, and immigrants, that is, all of those who are unlike the governing class.

The insistence of Israel's ancient covenant and the Jesus movement are to the contrary an advocacy for inclusion. Thus, Jesus broke every social barrier with reference to lepers, women, foreigners, and gentiles, as well as the "unclean." Eventually his movement will come to this attestation:

> *For he is our peace; in his flesh he has made both groups*
> *into one and has broken down the dividing wall, that is,*
> *the hostility between us. He has abolished the law with*
> *its commandments and ordinances, that he might create*
> *in himself one new humanity in place of the two, thus*
> *making peace, and might reconcile both groups to God*
> *in one body through the cross, thus putting to death that*
> *hostility through it. So he came and proclaimed peace to*
> *you who were far off and peace to those who were near;*
> *for through him both of us have access in one Spirit to the*
> *Father. So then you are no longer strangers and aliens,*
> *but you are citizens with the saints and also members of*
> *the household of God, built upon the foundation of the*
> *apostles and prophets, with Christ Jesus himself as the*
> *cornerstone. In him the whole structure is joined together*
> *and grows into a holy temple in the Lord; in him you also*
> *are built together spiritually into a dwelling place for God.*
> (Eph 2:14–22)

The breaking of the wall and the bridging of the gap between Jews and gentiles represents a whole new possibility in human history, one that echoes in every other reconciliation between those in and those out.

It is the sturdy advocacy of Desmond that the old regime of exclusion must and can be challenged and overcome. The walls of privilege and exclusion must be torn down to give access to the abundance that is the truth of our economy. Thus, he proposes "poverty abolition." He is a political realist. He understands that such an outcome cannot be a mere wish, but requires organized, sustained resolve, and action:

> *Behind every great blow dealt to the scourge of poverty,*
> *there have been ordinary Americans who have bound*
> *themselves to one another to accomplish extraordinary things.*
> *Social movements spark ideas, providing the blueprint for*
> *reform, as when the unemployed workers' movement of the*
> *late nineteenth century called for a public works program*
> *decades before the New Deal . . . Poverty will be abolished*
> *in America only when a mass movement demands it so.*
> *And today, such a movement stirs. American labor is once*
> *again on the move, growing more boisterous and feistier by*
> *the day, organizing workplaces once thought untouchable. A*
> *renewed movement for housing justice is gaining steam. In*
> *a resurgence of tenant power, renters have formed eviction*
> *blockades and chained themselves to the entrance of housing*
> *court, meeting the violence of displacement with a force of*
> *their own. The Poor People's Campaign has elevated the*
> *voices of low-income Americans around the country, voices*
> *challenging "the lie of scarcity in the midst of abundance"*
> *and mobilizing for things like educational equity and a*

> *reinvestment in public housing. They march under different*
> *banners—workers' unions and tenants' unions; movements*
> *for racial justice and economic justice—but they share a*
> *commitment to ending poverty in America.* (183–185)

Desmond sees that organized labor did the homework for the New Deal, that the civil rights movement caused and permitted the great congressional acts under Lyndon Johnson. He observes, "movements need people to march" (186). Those who march are those who have a vision of abundance, who have a hope of neighborliness, and who have a readiness for generosity. It is no wonder that in his final pages, Desmond mentions the Poor Peoples' Campaign and the leadership of William Barber. Such evocative energy is most likely to have theological grounding. We may imagine that the Moses movement and the Jesus movement were exactly grounded in the conviction of the extravagant generosity of the creator God.

It is, among other things, the good work of the church to insist upon the narrative of abundance, to reiterate in insistent ways the liturgy of abundance, and to interpret the ways in which such narrative and such liturgy together permit and require a different way in the world. That different, "more excellent" way in the world intends the breaking of all walls of exclusion. And that, in turn, requires a vigorous refutation of the well-grounded fears of scarcity that so beset us.

Thus, we must pay attention to the genres of our communities. On the one hand, we notice the *lists and categories* that classify and organize and exclude. On the other hand, there is the *praise and doxology* of self-abandonment. Such doxologies regularly run through and run over and run past every classification of insider and outsider. No wonder they were scandalized that he ate with sinners (Matt 9:10–13,

Mark 2:13–17, Luke 7:27–32). He willfully violated the long-running habits of exclusion. No wonder the apostle was dazzled when he wrote:

> *There is no longer Jew or Greek,*
> *there is no longer slave or free,*
> *there is no longer male or female,*
> *for all of you are one in Christ Jesus.* (Gal 3:28)

No wonder they were awed when the curtain in the temple was torn "from top to bottom," and they knew who he was (Matt 27:45–54, Mark 15:38–39, Luke 23: 44–49). No wonder!

6

GIVING UP

MY SIXTH APPEAL to Desmond concerns his recognition that the eradication of poverty in our society will require that those privileged and advantaged give up some things we treasure. In what may be the boldest page in this bold book, he writes:

> *Ending segregation, at last, would require affluent families to give up some things, but what we'd gain in return would be more valuable. We would have to* give up *the ways we hoard opportunity and public safety, but in doing so we'd also* give up *the shame that haunts us when we participate in the evil business of exclusion and poverty creation. We'd have to* give up *some comforts and familiarities of life behind the wall and* give up *the stories we've told ourselves about that place and our role in it, but we'd also be* giving up *the loneliness and empty materialism that have come to characterize much of upper-class life, allowing ourselves, in Baldwin's words, to reach "for higher dreams, for greater privileges."* (176–177; emphasis added)

Desmond advocates for the abolition of poverty, and believes it is a doable enterprise. But he is not a romantic. He is certain that wishful thinking and good intentions will not carry us very far without an alert social criticism and a strategy for the mobilization of social power. He sees that the abolition of poverty will require some concessions from the class of property, privilege, and advantage. Thus, his key paragraph is dominated by the imperative, "give up." The moneyed class must give up some of its leverage that has helped to produce and sustain the under-class of poverty. At the same time, Desmond sees that "giving up" is not simply a concession; it involves gains as well as losses. Thus, as one "gives up," one also gains. The requirement to "give up" concerns:

- the ways we hoard opportunity
- the ways we hoard public safety for ourselves
- some comforts and familiarities of life behind the wall
- the stories we tell ourselves about that place and our role in it, characteristically stories of success and self-sufficiency

But Desmond sees that along with such concessions, we could also at the same time:

- *give up the shame* we have for colluding in the creation of poverty and exclusion
- *give up the loneliness* that comes with money that isolates
- *give up the empty materialism*

These are no doubt trade-offs that could move us measurably toward "the pursuit of happiness."

A page later Desmond brings the issue of "giving up" close to his own life. He and his wife lived in a neighborhood in Milwaukee, Wisconsin. In that "mixed race, mixed income" community there was genuine community organized around a common garden. When the snow fell, neighbors cleared everyone's sidewalks. And then they relocated to a different neighborhood. It was a more affluent neighborhood, and no one helped any neighbor. Desmond reports on the requirement of his new neighborhood as a costly one,

> to give up *love for a community and trade a feeling of being known and held for the anomie of wealth. To us, that was a bad bargain.* (178)

Desmond's emphasis on "giving up"—positive and negative—led me to ponder the narrative of Jesus's encounter with a man who asked him about "eternal life" (Mark 10:17–31). Jesus provides two answers to his question. The first answer is that the man should obey the commandments of Torah:

> *You know the commandments: "You shall not murder; You shall not commit adultery; You shall not steal; You shall not bear false witness; You shall not defraud; Honor your father and mother."* (v. 19)

The man checks out okay on that front. But then Jesus gives a second answer:

> *You lack one thing; go, sell what you own, and give the money to the poor, and you will have treasure in heaven; then come, follow me.* (v. 21)

He invites the man to "follow," to walk the walk of the new regime that Jesus embodies and inaugurates. That new regime is one of transformed neighborliness. Participation in this new community requires being unburdened from wealth, power, and influence that are the common currency of "the old age." Thus, his imperative:

Go, sell, give, come, follow!

Divest! Yield the markers of worldly success. Give up one's standing in the world in order to participate in an alternative community where such standing counts for nothing. It is not a big surprise that the encounter ends tersely with this report:

He was shocked: He expected no such requirement beyond the commandments to be imposed on him. He was a good son of the Torah, who assumed that obedience to the commandments was the measure of a well-lived life. Jesus contradicted his carefully measured notion of virtue.

He was grieved: He had hoped for better. He was drawn to Jesus and his movement, but he had not realized that entering into that life required "giving up." He had not noted that the companions with Jesus were those who had no claims in the "old age."

He went away: He departed the company and the path of Jesus. He returned to the safer world where obedience to the commandments was sufficient for a well-lived life.

He had many possessions: Of course he did! He had many possessions, like all of us who live on the top side of power, affluence, and security. The man is a case study of the way in which the alternative society of the gospel, the one already initiated at Sinai, is in contradiction with our best vision of our present world. We have done our best to conceal that contradiction to prevent us from having to make hard choices that we do not want to make. Jesus puts a radical either/or before the man. I suggest it is the same either/or that Desmond offers about our choice for neighborliness, for the new world of Jesus is one of neighborly engagement, solidarity, and transformation.

As is usual for Jesus, his happenstance encounter with the shocked, grieving, departing man is an occasion for critical reflection with his followers. The disciples are being slowly schooled in their new life with him. Jesus says, having observed the man with many possessions:

> *How hard it will be for those who have wealth to enter the*
> *kingdom of God.* (Mark 10:23)

In the other gospel renditions, Jesus would observe that we cannot serve both God and money (Matt 6:24; Luke 16:13). This is what Jesus had made clear to the man, and what the man had understood all too well.

Mark reports that the disciples were "perplexed" at the deep either/or, but they did not say anything (v. 23). The either/or stunned them into silence. Jesus did not want to be misunderstood by them. He reiterated:

> *Children, how hard it is to enter the kingdom of God! It is*
> *easier for a camel to go through the eye of a needle than for*
> *someone who is rich to enter the kingdom of God.* (Mark
> 10:24–25)

How hard it is for a rich person to enter into the new community of Jesus! Harder than a camel in a needle's eye! Then the disciples get it; it will be really, really hard! In response to their consternation, Jesus offers something of an assurance. But it is not a cozy assurance:

> *For mortals it is impossible, but not for God; for God all*
> *things are possible.* (v. 27)

Begin with the recognition that it is impossible by human will or human resolve. That much the rich man had understood. But then,

> *With God all things are possible.*

God is God! God is all powerful. God can do the impossible. God has been doing the impossible since God gave a son to the aged Sarah and Abraham (Gen 18:14). The rich man had been too self-possessed and self-assured to recognize that something new could happen in his life that he had not decided on his own. But that is the mystery of human transformation. It is our human responsibility to "work out our own salvation with fear and trembling" (Phil 2:12). The rich man was seriously at work on that. He did not get the other part that it is "God who is at work in you, enabling you both to will and to work his good pleasure" (Phil 2:12–13). The part that is hidden from us is that "God is at work in you." It is for that reason that we may expect our lives to be transformed. It is for that reason that Desmond can hope that the moneyed can "give up" in order to move to real community. The mystery that the rich man did not compute is that his own will and effort toward well-being were penultimate. There is another purpose impinging upon our lives that summons and prods us—sometimes—to deep newness that we had never expected for ourselves.

The gospel narrative, however, adds a deep caveat to the claim that "God can do all things." In Mark 14:38, in his desperate, fearful prayer in the garden, Jesus affirms, "Father, for you all things are possible." Jesus reiterates an affirmation that is long-running in Israel (see Jer 32:17, 27). The narrative of Jesus in the garden makes one thing clear. It was *not possible* for Jesus, given who he was and what he intended, to avoid his fearful collision with establishment power that led to his execution. The power of God could not save him from the implications of his vocation. And as Jesus could not evade or avoid that dangerous "impossibility," so the rich man could not evade it, for it was *not possible* for the rich man to follow Jesus and bring all his wealth with him. Nor was it possible for the disciples. Thus, the rich man, the disciples, and those summoned by Desmond to "give up" are invited to ponder the impossibility of having it both ways, that is, retaining wealth along with the abolition of poverty. It is an either/or; it can never be a both/and.

Peter is alert to a "possibility": "Look!" He reminds Jesus that he has indeed "left everything," just what the rich man could not do. Peter, Andrew, James, and John had indeed abruptly abandoned their fishing business and their income. They had willingly, promptly, and without hesitation "followed." And before he finishes, Peter will indeed "give up" everything, including his life:

> But when you grow old, you will stretch out your hands, and someone else will fasten a belt around you and take you where you do not wish to go. (He said this to indicate the kind of death by which he would glorify God.) After this he said to him, "Follow me." (John 21:18–19)

In that final text in the fourth gospel, Jesus issues his same mandate
to Peter yet again: "Follow me" (v. 19). In Mark 10, Jesus responds to
Peter with a massive, comprehensive promise of restoration:

> *Truly I tell you, there is no one who has left house or brothers*
> *or sisters or mother or father or children or fields, for my*
> *sake and for the sake of the good news, who will not receive*
> *a hundredfold now in this age—houses, brothers and sisters,*
> *mothers and children, and fields with persecutions—and in*
> *the age to come eternal life.* (vv. 29–30)

Jesus provides for Peter a catalog of "everything": family and fields . . . a
hundredfold! But he adds two provisos. First, the "giving up" must be for
the sake of Jesus and for the sake of the good news. Jesus is not impressed
with "giving up" that is not in the service of hope for new possibility. Second,
the wondrous future will be given "with persecutions." Nothing easy about
passage to the new regime! Thus, Jesus's reassurance to Peter for his ready
obedience is mixed and qualified. Jesus knows, well beyond the horizon of
Peter, that that gain through "giving up" is not an easy gain judged by the
norms of the world. The anticipation Desmond has for those who "give up"
for the sake of the abolition of poverty is like that. It is not a gain judged
by the old norms of wealth and power. It is a gain only if our new life in
community can be treasured beyond our old norms of well-being.

And then Jesus adds a zinger that is his trademark:

> *first . . . last*
> *exalted . . . humbled*
> *lost . . . found*
> *empty . . . full* (v. 31)

So what about the restoration of "a hundredfold?" The restoration will not be of the old variety. The restoration will, perhaps, be held in common. There will be a new family of glad obedience; there will be restored fields held in common; there will be flourishing communities of the vulnerable in which the now "emptied" can gladly participate. The contest between the offer of Jesus and the hope of the rich is breathtaking. While Desmond would likely not articulate the abolition of poverty in such radical or demanding terms, his bid is quite like this gospel offer. Jesus, and Desmond after him, offers an either/or that is deeply uncompromising.

By the time we reach the apostolic counsel of Paul to his congregation in Corinth, the radicality of this either/or of Jesus has been toned down. But Paul still summons the congregation to "give up" of itself for the sake of the common good of the church. In 2 Corinthians 8, Paul bids the congregation to submit a generous offering for the sake of other congregations in dire straits. He grounds his appeal to the church in an affirmation that "our Lord Jesus Christ" gave up his "richness" for the sake of others:

> *For you know the generous act of our Lord Jesus Christ, that*
> *though he was rich, yet for your sakes he became poor, so that*
> *by his poverty you might become rich.* (2 Cor 8:9)

The point is an echo from Paul's earlier appeal to the Philippian hymn:

> *Though he was in the form of God,*
> *did not regard equality with God as something to be exploited,*
> *but emptied himself,*
> *taking the form of a slave,*

being born in human likeness.
And being found in human form,
  he humbled himself and became obedient to the point of
    death—
even death on a cross. (Phil 2:6–7)

Jesus is the pacesetter and example for the church to "give" of itself for the sake of others. In his realism Paul acknowledges that such generosity in the church will have limits:

> *Now finish doing it, so that your eagerness may be matched*
> *by completing it according to your means . . . I do not mean*
> *that there should be relief for others and pressure on you,*
> *but it is a question of a fair balance between your present*
> *abundance and their need, so that their abundance may*
> *be for your need, in order that there may be a fair balance.*
> (2 Cor 8:11–14)

But his quotation from the manna story in verse 15 indicates that the generosity of each one can create an economy of shared abundance (see Exod 16:18). He urges his congregation to "excel in this generous undertaking" (v. 7). Thus, the church—the Christian congregation—unlike the world is a community that gives and gives up in response to the needs of others, propelled by the example of self-giving that Jesus carried to extremity. Thus, the habit of the church in giving and in self-giving is a quite countercultural habit, for the way of the world is to acquire, to hoard, and to accumulate to monopoly—so "bigger barns" and "storehouse cities." But not the church! Thus, the giving and giving up of the church is not simply an in-house enterprise in order to maintain the church in its mission. It is also a public responsibility to invest and bet on public practices and public policies that allow the common community to prosper. As poverty is caused by the predatory inclination of the powerful, so poverty can be abolished by the processes of giving and giving up in order to overcome the usual habits of our economy.

Desmond finishes his exposition with a compelling summons:

> *Every person, every company, every institution that has a role in perpetuating poverty also has a role in ameliorating it. The end of poverty is something to stand for, to march for, to sacrifice for. Because poverty is the dream killer, the capability destroyer, the great waster of human potential. It is a misery and a national disgrace, one that belies any claim to our greatness. The citizens of the richest nation in the world can and should finally put an end to it.* (189)

But then I was stopped short by his final sentences:

> *We don't need to outsmart this problem. We need to out-hate it.* (189)

His penultimate word is "hate." Hate the problem. Hate the reality of poverty. Hate the economic practices that sanction such poverty. His word, "hate," struck me as astonishingly strong, a measure of how clearly he feels the issue, and how urgently he regards the solution. But then I remembered that the same term was on the lips of Jesus:

No one can serve two masters; for a slave will either hate the
one and love the other, or be devoted to the one and despise
the other. You cannot serve God and wealth. (Matt 6:24;
Luke 16:13)

Whoever comes to me and does not hate father and mother,
wife and children, brothers and sisters, yes, and even life
itself, cannot be my disciples. (Luke 14:26)

The term "hate" is not in the parallel in Matthew, but the point is the
same:

For I have come to set a man against his father,
and a daughter against her mother,
and a daughter-in-law against her mother-in-law;
and ones' foes will be members of one's own household.
Whoever loves father or mother more than me is not worthy of
    me; and whoever loves son or daughter more than me is not
    worthy of me; and whoever does not take up the cross and
    follow me is not worthy of me. Those who find their life will
    lose it, and those who lose their life for my sake will find it.
    (Matt 10:35–39)

Jesus refuses an easy both/and for the sake of one's family. Desmond's
insistence is with the same either/or of urgency, either business as usual
with an abiding poverty-class, or a new deployment of resources so
that the poor can participate in the shaping of their own futures.

What better finish for me than the great hymn "God of Grace
and God of Glory" by Harry Emerson Fosdick:

Cure thy children's warring madness; bend our pride to thy
    control;
Shame our wanton selfish gladness, rich in things and poor in
    soul.
Grant us wisdom, grant us courage,
Lest we miss thy kingdom's goal, lest we miss thy kingdom's goal.
(Glory to God, 307)

This third stanza of the hymn is a prayer and petition in three parts:

- cure . . . because we cannot help ourselves
- bend . . . because we are stiff-necked in stubbornness
- shame . . . our self-indulgent self-sufficiency

Note that Desmond comments on "the shame that haunts us when we participate in the usual business of exclusion and poverty creation" (p. 177). The shame we may rightly expect before the holy God is because we are, so the hymn goes, "rich in things . . . poor in soul." This was exactly the situation of the rich man in Mark 10. He had no "soul," no capacity for resonance with the Holy God. Consequently, he over-valued his "things" in which he was rich.

Fosdick voices two more petitions in the stanza:

- Give us wisdom
- Give us courage

Give us wisdom and courage for "thy kingdom's goal" which is a neigh-borhood of neighbor schooled in hospitality, generosity, and forgive-ness. Such practices require the courage to be upstream in a culture of greed. They also require wisdom to see how best to work effectively to transform the economy. So, imagine the church with its continuing petitions: "Cure, bend, shame." And then imagine the church with wisdom and courage for the sake of God's new rule. The rich man could not get there; we, however, are left in the good company of Peter who left everything and followed, followed because he had opted out of the old regime of greed and violence.

❦ 7 ❧

COVETING

IN THIS SERIES of reflections on Matthew Desmond's *Poverty, by America*, I have considered some ways in which his strong analysis and advocacy concerning poverty and social well-being have compelling counterpoints in the witness of Scripture. I have no doubt that exploration of the interface between the testimony of Scripture and contemporary critical work on social reality is an important undertaking. It is important because it exhibits ways in which our faith can impinge upon our understanding of, and response to, present social reality. It is equally important because it permits us to read and discern the Bible in a way connected to real-world issues, and thus resists any effort at an other-worldly take on the Bible. My understanding of Desmond's advocacy leads me to articulate in three parts (what else!) the large drama of human freedom, responsibility, possibility, and decision-making.

First, in the liturgical imagination of ancient Israel, there was a season at the outset of creation for "original blessing" that was unmarred by any contradiction of the will of the creator. Thus, the wondrously symmetrical account of creation in Genesis 1:1–2:4 is offered before any of the subsequent troubles of the earliest creatures. All is peaceable, harmonious, and generative. That sum of well-being is happily voiced in the lyrical articulation of the God of the whirlwind:

> *Where were you when I laid the foundation of the earth?*
> *Tell me, if you have understanding.*
> *Who determined its measurements—surely you know!*
> *Or who stretched the line upon it?*
> *On what were its bases sunk,*
> *or who laid its cornerstone*
> *when the morning stars sang together*
> *and all the heavenly beings shouted for joy?* (Job 38:4–7)

The poetry characterizes a "before time" before human understanding or human undertaking. That "before time" is marked by lyrical joy in heaven. Imagine all the stars and moon and sun shout together for joy! What else could they do, so beside themselves in elation at the beauty and wonder and goodness of creation? Job cannot answer because he, like all of us, has no access to that "before time." Thus, the great hymnic Psalms (e.g., 147, 148, 150) portray all the creatures gathered together in glad praise. They must sing because they cannot "say." They cannot utter reasonable sentences about this reality because its splendor defies and outruns rational utterance, and so song, hymn, praise, elation, joy!

Second, we know better and the Bible knows better. We have at hand no such blessed world. Rather, what we have at hand is a world filled with *vigorous contradiction* marked by fear, greed, and violence. The world is like that all around us. The Bible is not much into explanation. It tells stories of the contradiction that classical theology labels "the fall." But the Bible does not linger over the label. It gives us,

- the rebellious story of Adam and Eve (Gen 3)
- the lethal story of Cain and Abel (Gen 4)

- the covetousness of David (2 Sam 11)
- the willfulness of Jeroboam (1 Kgs 11-12)
- the violence of Jezebel and Ahab (1 Kgs 21)

That, plus a myriad of other narratives about life that contradicts the good will of the creator, stories ancient and stories contemporary, all attest to *fear* at our human limit, *greed* to overcome the fear, and *violence* to advance and enforce the greed. Such a sequence of fear, greed, and violence is in every detail a refusal of the "original blessing" of God. And if we accept the phrase "original blessing," then we can entertain the old misleading phrase, "original sin." It is sin in principle, since the world lives in resistance to the good offer of God's blessing.

The source of such trouble is a deep enigma to us. In the primary narrative of the first couple, the "cause" of the disruption is, on the one hand, the lure and seduction that comes from a slippery, slimy creature; on the other hand, the first couple must answer for it:

> *So when the woman saw that the tree was good for food, and that it was a delight to the eyes, and that the tree was to be desired to make one wise, she took of its fruit and ate; and she also gave some to her husband, who was with her, and he ate.* (Gen 3:6)

The operational word is "desire." The narrative does not say that the first couple "desired," nothing that active. It says that the tree was "desired." Clearly "desire" is at the heart of the tale. The term *hamad* is in many other places in Scripture translated as "covet," that is, a desire that is inappropriate and unfitting. Here the tree of knowledge is inappropriate because the Lord of the garden had forbidden it. But the desire overrides the divine prohibition. The first couple eats it anyway. Perhaps they could not help themselves, so powerful are our illicit desires. We may conclude that this "desire," however it came to be, is a misguided yearning because it violates the terms of interaction between creator and creature. Thus, we may judge the forfeiture of "original blessing" is credited to an inappropriate but powerful desire that readily violates that defining connection.

The Bible provides rich reflection on the immense power of covetousness, that is, inappropriate desire. In an early (primitive) narrative, it is reported that Israel lost a military battle because of trouble in the community (Josh 7:2–5). When Joshua sought an explanation for the rout, this was the divine answer:

> *Israel has sinned; they have transgressed my covenant that I*
> *imposed on them. They have taken some of the devoted things;*
> *they have stolen, they have acted deceitfully, and they have*
> *put them among their own belongings.* (Josh 7:11)

Joshua's investigation of the affront leads to a sin committed by Achan of the tribe of Judah. When confronted, Achan confessed:

> *It is true; I am the one who sinned against the Lord God*
> *of Israel. This is what I did: when I saw among the spoil a*
> *beautiful mantle from Shinar, and two hundred shekels of*
> *silver, and a bar of gold weighing fifty shekels, then I coveted*
> *them and took them. They now lie hidden in the ground*
> *inside my tent, with the silver underneath.* (Josh 7:20-21)

He coveted shiny valuable objects. His coveting brought immense trouble on the community.

The royal history of Israel is marred at the outset by the concupiscence of David:

> *David sent someone to inquire about the woman . . . So*
> *David sent messengers to get her, and she came to him, and*
> *he lay with her.* (2 Sam 11:3–4)

The narrative does not use the term "covet." But it does use the strong verb "take" that has been softened in translation. The term suggests an act of violent usurpation (see 2 Sam 12:9).

In the prophetic tradition the reality of coveting takes on a more realistic practice of craving for and usurping the property of others:

> *Alas for those who devise wickedness and evil deeds on their beds!*
> *When the morning dawns, they perform it,*
> *because it is in their power.*
> *They* covet *fields, and seize* them;
> *Houses, and take them away;*
> *they oppress householder and house,*
> *people and their inheritance.* (Mic 2:1–2)

These poetic lines describe a quite forceful, insistent, credible economic process through which the powerful confiscate the real estate of the vulnerable "because it is in their power." In prophetic horizon such violation of neighborliness does not go unanswered, but will eventually result in the displacement of the acquisitive:

> *Therefore thus says the Lord:*
> *Now, I am devising against this family an evil from which you*
> *cannot remove your necks;*

and you shall not walk haughtily,
for it will be an evil time.
On that day they shall take up a taunt song against you,
and wail with bitter lamentation,
and say, "We are utterly ruined;
the Lord alters the inheritance of my people;
how he removes it from me!
Among our captors he parcels out our fields."
Therefore you will have no one to cast the line
by lot in the assembly of the Lord (Mic 2:3–5)

What is an inexplicable act by the first couple, and an incidental act by Achan in prophetic horizon is a systemic act that leads to displacement and disruption of community possibility. Thus, Isaiah can describe the same acquisitiveness by the powerful that can only result in the failure of the agricultural economy:

Ah, you who join house to house,
who add field to field,
until there is no room for no one but you,
and you are left to live alone in the midst of the land!
The Lord of hosts has sworn in my hearing:
Surely many houses shall be desolate,
large and beautiful houses, without inhabitant.
For ten acres of vineyard shall yield but one bath,
and a homer of seed shall yield a mere ephah. (Isa 5:8–10)

D. N. Premnath, in his comment on the verses, *Eighth Century Prophets: A Social Analysis* (2003), writes:

It is noteworthy that verse 10 lists two major items of export from Palestine: wine and grain. These items were exported in exchange for luxury and strategic military items. Thus, the local economic resources went to support the elite and their lifestyle. The primary producers benefitted in no way from the fruits of their labor. The firm control of the distributive process by the ruling elite was responsible for this. The judgment speaks of depriving the rich of the very things of which they had deprived the peasants. (102)

It cannot go unnoticed that the commandments at Sinai culminate with a twice repeated "covet":

You shall not covet your neighbor's house; you shall not covet your neighbor's wife, or male or female slave, or ox, or donkey, or anything that belongs to your neighbor. (Exod 20:17; Deut 5:21)

The catalog of the prohibition is comprehensive:

House, wife, slave, ox, donkey . . . anything!

Coveting is a violation of neighborliness. Thus, the Bible readily links together *the hidden force of inappropriate desire* and *the practical real-world acquisitiveness* of such a desire that does damage to the community. Desmond's characterization of poverty is exactly a reiteration of the destructive force of coveting wherein the powerful and privileged hoard for themselves the resources that properly belong to the entire community. Perhaps the ultimate insistence concerning "coveting" is in the epistle:

> *Put to death, therefore, whatever in you is earthly:*
> *fornication, impurity, passion, evil desire, and greed (which is*
> *idolatry).* (Col 3:5)

The older translation had "covetousness" that in NRSV has rendered as "greed." Thus, *covetousness* is equivalent to *idolatry*. Inappropriate desire is tantamount to the worship of false gods. An economy of acquisitiveness that is willing and able to violate vulnerable neighbors is the embrace of a false world presided over by false gods that cannot save. Desmond's advocacy is precisely a summons away from a false world of self-sufficiency that is propelled by a deep fear of inadequacy and insecurity, of never having enough yet that would make one safer and more sufficient. It is possible to trace such an oppressive economy from the strictures of Micah to the forceful analysis of Desmond. That account from Micah to Matthew (Desmond) would run exactly through the "laws of enclosure" in eighteenth-century England through which owners of landed estates prevented the poor of the community from foraging for wood and food from their land. (See Karl Polyani, *The Great Transformation* [1944]). In passing it is worth notice that the first writing of Karl Marx concerned exactly such laws of exclusion that protected private property from public use, and so denied the vulnerable the resources required for their livelihood.

Third, we are left with the reality of a memory (and a hope!) for *a creation of harmony*, which in the will of the creator is without contestation and *an economy of greed* that pits neighbor against neighbor. This interface is the great either/or of covenantal-prophetic-evangelical faith that is most clearly articulated by Jeremiah:

> *Thus says the Lord: Do not let the wise boast in their wisdom, do not let the mighty boast in their might, do not let the wealthy boast in their wealth; but let those who boast boast in this, that they understand and know me, that I am the Lord; I act with steadfast love, justice, and righteousness in the earth, for in these things I delight, says the Lord.* (Jer 9:23–24)

The prophet articulates two triads of practice. On the one hand a practice that asserts self-sufficiency and self-possessiveness:

> *Wisdom, might, wealth.*

On the other hand, a triad of neighborly practices that are grounded in the delight of the creator:

> *Steadfast love, justice, and righteousness.*

In the rhetoric of the prophet, this is an either/or that admits of no softening or compromise. One cannot have it both ways, try as we will. Likewise, in the rhetoric of Desmond, it is an either/or concerning *predatory wealth* that produces and sustains poverty, or a *reallocation of resources* to permit the poor a stake in the wealth of the community.

Biblical faith, with its critique of private wealth and its advocacy of the public good, is indeed a summons to redecide. It is a call for a decision that is congruous with the creator God, and a refusal of the

contrary. While I have cited examples of inappropriate desire contrary
to the creator God, we might consider the simple trust of the Psalmist:

> *One thing I asked of the Lord, that will I seek after:*
> *to live in the house of the Lord all the days of my life,*
> *and to behold the beauty of the Lord,*
> *and to inquire in his temple.* (Ps 27:4)

The Psalmist hopes for only one thing, to live in the presence of God.
And in covenantal Israel, life in the presence of God is inescapably life
with the neighbor. Israel could not anticipate life with the God of the
covenant without reference to the neighbor.

> *So when you are offering your gift at the altar, if you*
> *remember that your brother or sister has something against*
> *you, leave your gift there before the altar and go; first be*
> *reconciled to your brother or sister, and then come and offer*
> *your gift.* (Matt 5:23–24)

Just as Desmond's book bids that we should redecide about
poverty, wealth, and neighbor, so the Bible is a long, insistent summons
to the same decision. We may notice three dramatic moments in that
long-running summons:

1. Moses sets before Israel "two ways" along with an imperative to
   decide:

   > *See, I have set before you today life and prosperity, death*
   > *and adversity . . . Choose life so that you and your*

*descendants may live, loving the Lord your God, obeying
him, and holding fast to him; for that means life to you and
length of days.* (Deut 30:15, 19–20)

2. Joshua summons Israel to choose between Yahweh and other
gods, and warns against any easy or glib decision:

*Now if you are unwilling to serve the Lord, choose this day
whom you will serve, whether the gods your ancestors served
in the region beyond the River or the gods of the Amorites in
whose land you are living; but as for me and my household,
we will serve the Lord . . . Then put away the foreign gods
that are among you, and incline your hearts to the Lord, the
God of Israel.* (Josh 24:15, 23)

3. Jesus offers his disciples "two paths" and warns that one is much
harder than the other:

*Enter through the narrow gate; for the gate is wide and the
road is easy that leads to destruction, and there are many
who take it. For the gate is narrow and the road is hard that
leads to life, and there are few who find it.* (Matt 7:13–14)

Desmond's book on poverty and abundance follows in the train
of these imperatives. Desmond sees, as clearly as Moses, Joshua, and
Jesus, that a choice against neighborliness is a choice that in the long
run ends in calamity. His shrewd analysis shows the deep claims of
faith and life come down to the specificity of the neighbor and an
economy of generosity. It is no different in the catalog of Paul:

> *By contrast, the fruit of the Spirit is love, joy, peace, patience, kindness, generosity, faithfulness, gentleness, and self-control. There is no law against such things.* (Gal 5:22–23)

We decide about such possibilities via our practices of policy, election, and budget. Such venues for decision-making tell powerfully about the futures we may choose for ourselves and for our neighbors.

CONCLUSION

Poverty in the Land of Promise

IT IS EVIDENT that most people in our society, across the political spectrum, are inclined to be generous toward neighbors. This is manifest in ready responses to serious crises and in cases of special dramatic need. It is clear in our common readiness to crowd-source all "sorts and conditions" of people who face special costly circumstances. That evident generosity, however, is (also across the political spectrum) fully encased in an ideology of capitalism that believes that wealth is private and that our neighbors are also competitors for limited resources. Practically, that deep commitment to capitalism is expressed as trust in the market that has come to dominate the economy through an ideology of individualism.

It has become increasingly self-evident that the market should no longer be viewed as an institution that must be regulated by external forces, but, on the contrary, it should be used to regulate society as a whole. The market thus becomes the leading principle for guiding individual and collective action. We are confronted with a clear distinction between the market as a public place and the market as a principle for regulating social relations (see "Market" by Gerald Berthoud, in *The Development Dictionary: A Guide to Knowledge as Power*, 2nd ed., edited by Wolfgang Sachs, New York: Zed Books, 2010, 74, 79).

Thus, while we may practice generosity face-to-face by way of charity, in terms of larger public reality, our generosity shrivels before the need for self-benefit and selfish well-being. The outcome of such generosity within an ideology of greed is that the public domain suffers and those without leverage are noticeably and visibly left behind. The task before us, as I have suggested in following the wisdom of Matthew Desmond, is that the vice-grip of unregulated capitalism must be challenged through the offer of an alternative economy. That alternative is insistently offered in the testimony of Scripture. The defining event in the memory of ancient Israel, the Exodus event, was not a walk in the woods or a tea party. It was, rather, a risky, dramatic, determined confrontation between the established socio-economic power of the empire (embodied by Pharaoh) and those who were kept in slave labor to serve Pharaoh's monopoly. At the behest of the emancipatory God who intervened in the economics of Pharaoh, the "mixed multitude" of peasant slaves refused Pharaoh's systemic exploitation. That daring company arrived at Mount Sinai where Moses boldly articulated an alternative economics that is grounded in his tenth commandment, "Thou shalt not covet" (Exod 20:17). Moses insisted that this terse command be etched in clay tablets as it is etched in the fabric of creation. This visionary articulation of Moses is subsequently reinforced by the urgency of the prophetic tradition and by the discerning shrewdness of the wisdom tradition. In every such voice—Moses, the prophets, the wisdom teachers—there is the insistent covenantal conviction that neighbor practice must preempt private predatory gain.

And of course, the Jesus movement in the New Testament reasserts the Mosaic vision of the economy. Twice Jesus lays down his marker concerning economic conviction and practice: "No one can serve two masters; for a slave will either hate the one and love the other, or be devoted to the one and despise the other. You cannot serve God and wealth" (Matt 6:24; see Luke 16:13). The God to be served, according to this statement, is the emancipatory God of Moses who is the covenant-making God of Sinai. The alternative to "wealth" (mammon, capital) is a recognition that a commitment to money-making, money-taking, and money-coveting practices is elementally inimical to the God of the gospel. After all, Jesus was not executed by the empire because he dressed or talked funny. He was executed by the state because he posed a serious threat to its economic ideology.

For good reason the Bible—both the Moses community and the Jesus community—recognize that "coveting" for private gain at the expense of the public good is a disaster. In the Old Testament the point is clearly made in the crisis caused by Achan that brought catastrophe on his community. Achan belatedly confesses to Joshua:

> *I am the one who sinned against the Lord God of Israel.*
> *This is what I did; when I saw among the spoil a beautiful*
> *mantle from Shinar, and two hundred shekels of silver, and*
> *a bar of gold weighing fifty shekels, then I coveted them and*
> *took them. They now lie hidden in the ground inside my tent,*
> *with the silver underneath.* (Josh 7:20–21)

The point is likewise made in the New Testament. The narrative of Acts 5:1–11 reports on how trouble came when a member of the community withheld wealth from the community. Neither Ananias nor Sapphira, the perpetrators, had a chance to testify, because in both their cases they are immediately struck dead at the accusation: He kept back some of the proceeds (of a sale of property), and brought only part of it and laid it at the apostle's feet (Acts 5:2).

It is no wonder that the epistle writer can conclude that "Greed is idolatry," the embrace of false gods (Col 3:5)! Thus, we are able to see the profound either/or between an economy based on private gain or greed and a covenantal economy grounded in the public good. This either/or is stark and unaccommodating. It is the work of the synagogue and the church that treasure this biblical text to make the point clearly as it pertains to our present economic crisis of excessive wealth alongside unbearable need. It is my judgment that these text-based communities must muster the courage and honesty to face the contradiction between these two economies with some directness. The matter is urgent because all of us in faith communities—liberal and conservative—live amid this contradiction that so defines our daily life.

Of course, in actual practice the matter is inescapably difficult. It is difficult because we rarely have sufficient conviction to enunciate the claims of faith. It is difficult beyond that because in actual practice matters are extremely complex and complicated. Thus, the bold either/or of faith must be factored out in actual practice by the enactment of policies and regulations that of necessity are compromises. Clearly this either/or in some form matters compellingly beyond the confines of these two biblical communities. That is, those who do not share the claims of these particular texts must inescapably face the same crisis concerning the enigma of the public good and private interests. It has been tempting and easy for the church to reach a long-running settlement of the public/private matter by accenting charity as the work of private good while at the same time remaining silent about public matters while the market works its ruthless will. But such a bifurcation does not finally work, because it yields a major disconnect between faith and actual lived reality. Thus, in the face of our current economic crisis, our work is to show how and in what ways the claims of covenantal economics are indispensable for our public practice. This will require the church (at the local level) to do the work of teaching and interpretation that it has too often failed to do.

While we do not and cannot expect our secular, multi-dimensioned society to adhere specifically to our claims of faith, we can anticipate that the claims of faith in matters economic can and must be taken seriously in the public conversation and in the formation of policy. The recurring problem has not been resistance of public engagement but the cowardice of the church in voicing its conviction. I fully anticipate that we are at a new moment when the church can articulate a faith perspective on the economy that will receive a serious hearing in our society, because these claims ring true in the actual human community. As Elijah discovered when he felt alone and bereft in his hard assignment, there are "still 7,000" who have not sold out (1 Kgs 19:18). The number is elastic. There are great numbers of folk, in church and in the synagogue and beyond both of these communities, who care intensely about these neighborly matters. The work is to gather such a company into political energy of a transformative ilk.